THE GIANT BOOK OF
DINOSAURS

This edition first published 1992 by Dean,
an imprint of Reed International Books Ltd.,
Michelin House, 81 Fulham Road, London SW3 6RB

Copyright © 1988 Octopus Books Limited

ISBN 0 603 55106 8

Printed in Hungary

THE GIANT BOOK OF
DINOSAURS

A COLOURFUL GUIDE TO THE FASCINATING
WORLD OF THE DINOSAURS

WRITTEN BY DR MICHAEL BENTON
ILLUSTRATED BY MARTIN KNOWELDEN

DEAN

CONTENTS

FINDING THE EVIDENCE
How were dinosaurs first discovered?

Huge bones of dinosaurs were first found in England over 300 years ago. At first nobody knew what they were. They thought the bones might have come from elephants.

Then, in 1822, something happened to change this. A Mrs Mantell was walking near her home in the country, when she spotted what looked like an enormous tooth lying in a pile of rubble. She took the tooth and showed it to her husband, Gideon Mantell, who was a doctor and also a keen geologist in his spare time. (A geologist studies rocks and fossils.)

He showed the tooth to experts in London. Some of them told him that it came from a great fish. Others said that it came from a rhinoceros. Finally, someone said that it was just like the tooth of an iguana lizard, only it was much bigger.

The Mantells collected more teeth and bones from this animal, and in 1825 Gideon Mantell named it *Iguanodon*, which means 'iguana-tooth'.

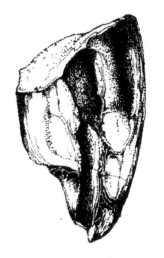

Left: the tooth of *Iguanodon* found by Mrs Mantell in 1822. It was one of the first dinosaur 'fossils' to be discovered. (A fossil is the remains of an animal or plant that once lived on the earth.)

Above: Mrs Mantell, and a sketch by Gideon Mantell of what he thought *Iguanodon* looked like. He thought it was a giant lizard about 60 metres (180 feet) long.

Main scene: the picture is based on a reconstruction made by Sir Richard Owen in 1853. He thought *Iguanodon* was a massive four-legged dinosaur with a horn on its nose like a rhinoceros.

Left: a modern reconstruction shows that *Iguanodon* actually had two legs and no horn. We now know that what Owen thought was a horn was in fact one of its sharp thumbs!

Bone wars

Right: Othniel Marsh (back row, right) and one of his teams of dinosaur-bone collectors. They had to be heavily armed because of unfriendly Indians, as well as rival bone collectors!

Below: some giant bones of *Apatosaurus* are discovered in Wyoming, USA.

Some of the most famous dinosaurs were found and collected in the western USA between 1870 and 1900.

The collectors were often tough armed men, and they worked in very hard conditions. Most of the bone-digging crews were paid by one of two men: either Edward Cope of Philadelphia, Pennsylvania, or Othniel Marsh of New Haven, Connecticut. These two were deadly rivals, and competed to find the most new dinosaurs.

They sent their teams to Montana, Colorado and Wyoming, where they worked through the year digging up bones. The bones they dug up were then packed in great crates, and hauled by horse and cart to the nearest railway station. From there they were sent east and hurriedly unpacked.

Cope or Marsh then raced to name the new dinosaurs that had just arrived. The name published first was the name that stuck and the one everyone would use. Sometimes there was only a few days between Cope and Marsh announcing the same new discoveries. So the new dinosaur would often get two different names. Between them, Cope and Marsh named many important dinosaurs, like *Allosaurus, Apatosaurus (Brontosaurus), Diplodocus, Stegosaurus,* and *Triceratops,* for example. New dinosaurs are still being discovered today all over the world.

Below: important new dinosaurs are still being found. *Baryonyx,* **or 'heavy claw', from the south of England, was named in 1986.**

New discovery of dinos

A claw, a finger and a humerus bone from an from and has been named *Baryonyx walkeri,*

Below: dinosaurs have been found in nearly every part of the world.

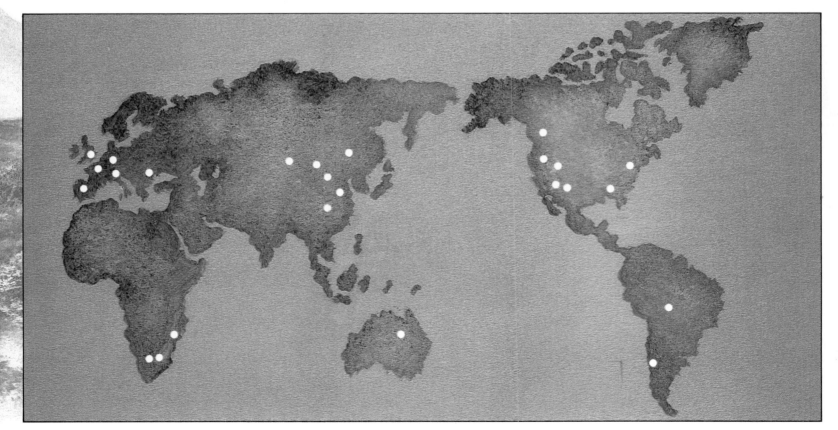

Fossils

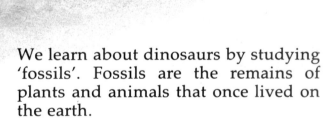

Right: preparing the skeleton of the giant *Camarasaurus*. A technician is carefully removing the rock from the bones of a giant dinosaur at the famous Dinosaur National Monument in Colorado, USA.

Below: dinosaur trackways, showing the shape of the foot, the long pointed toes, and the length of the stride.

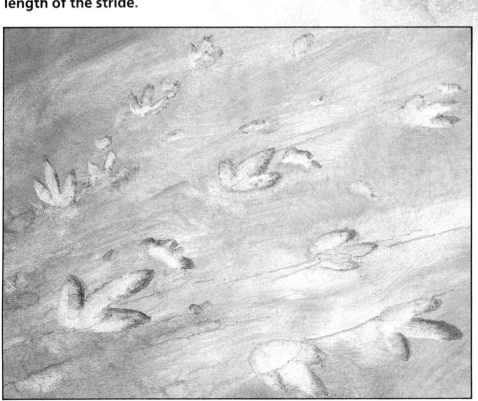

We learn about dinosaurs by studying 'fossils'. Fossils are the remains of plants and animals that once lived on the earth.

Bones

Generally we can only tell about the hard parts of a plant or animal from fossils. Usually only the bones of dinosaurs become fossils, because the flesh and soft tissues all rot away. Over many thousands of years the bones become filled with chemicals that harden. A fossil bone is usually heavy, just like a stone. But all of the detail can usually still be seen on the surface of the bone, and also inside it. Inside bones there are different fibres and structures which can usually be seen when a fossil bone is cut across.

Soft tissue

Sometimes, fossils of the soft parts of an animal are also found. For example, woolly mammoths (large extinct elephants) have been found frozen, just as they were, in northern Russia. Scientists have even eaten their flesh, although it probably didn't taste very good! But dinosaur fossils are much older than mammoth fossils and the only soft parts of dinosaurs that have been found are very rare marks left by their skin, which show the pattern of the scales.

Quite often dinosaur footprints and trackways have been found. The fossil footprints may be very detailed, and can show the exact shape of the foot, the claw marks, and even the folds of the scaly skin. When a dinosaur ran across some wet sand, it made clear footprints, which were often covered with more mud or sand and then turned to rock. Scientists can also measure the length of a dinosaur's stride from a trackway, and then work out how fast it was running.

Left: how a fossil is formed.

The body of a dead dinosaur sinks to the bottom of a river or lake. It may be washed along by the current, and partly covered by mud.

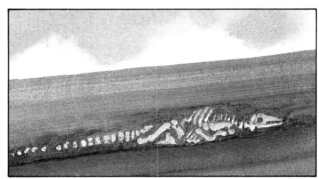

Small animals eat the flesh of the dinosaur, and the rest of the soft tissue rots away. Only the bony skeleton is left. This is soon covered by soft mud or sand.

Over time, the mud and sand turn into rock. After millions of years, the landscape changes, and the bed of the river or lake bed rises.

The rock is worn away by the wind and rain, and parts of the skeleton appear. Someone walking past may pick up pieces of bone. A team of scientists from a museum can then come to dig the skeleton up.

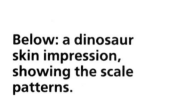

Below: a dinosaur skin impression, showing the scale patterns.

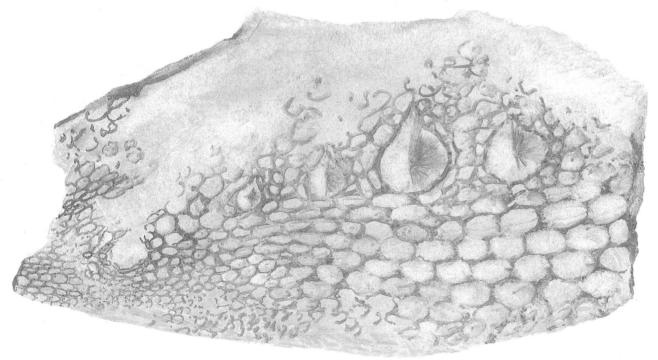

11

Discovering dinosaurs

Right: the skeleton of a dinosaur has been discovered. It may take weeks to remove all the rock above it. Fine chisels and brushes have to be used to avoid damaging the bones.

Far right: the bones are protected with bandages soaked in plaster. This forms a hard shell all around each block.

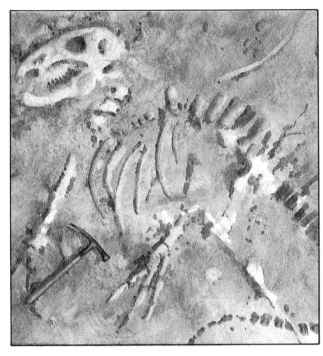

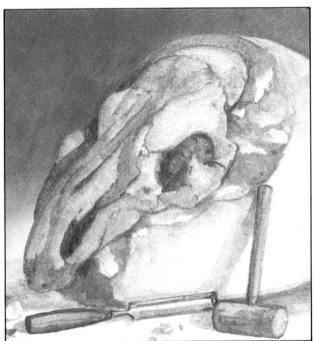

Right: the blocks are carefully numbered so that the scientists know where each part came from.

Left: back in the laboratory, the plaster cast is carefully cut away and the bones are cleaned. This may take many weeks of work. The bone may be hardened with special plastics to prevent decay.

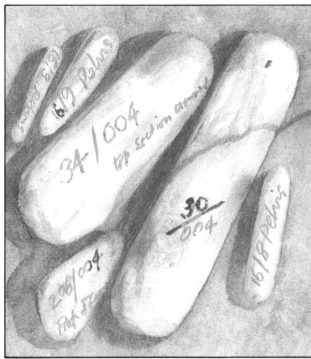

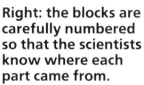

Right: the bones are fixed to strong metal frames which can hold the weight of the bones.

Far right: if the skeleton is a good one, it may be mounted in the museum for everyone to see.

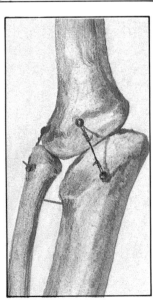

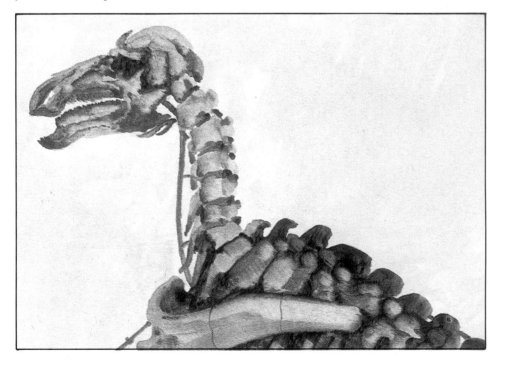

Digging up dinosaurs

Many dinosaur skeletons have been dug up in the past 100 years. It takes a long time to 'excavate', or dig up, a dinosaur because they are usually very big, and the diggers have to be careful not to damage the bones.

When a skeleton is found, the whole area has to be cleared. Then the rock is carefully removed from above the skeleton. The bones are protected from damage as far as possible with plaster casts. Then the excavators have to get underneath the bones and tip them over to clean the other side. The skeleton of an ordinary dinosaur can weigh 10 to 20 tonnes.

Left: first the skeleton is reconstructed.

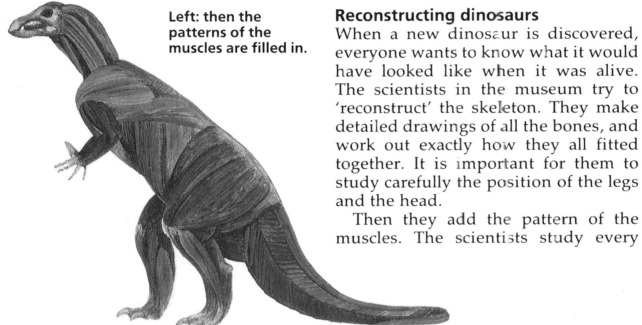

Left: then the patterns of the muscles are filled in.

Reconstructing dinosaurs

When a new dinosaur is discovered, everyone wants to know what it would have looked like when it was alive. The scientists in the museum try to 'reconstruct' the skeleton. They make detailed drawings of all the bones, and work out exactly how they all fitted together. It is important for them to study carefully the position of the legs and the head.

Then they add the pattern of the muscles. The scientists study every bone to find out where the muscles attached. Each muscle moves one part of the body, and the size of a muscle shows how strong it was. You can see that this dinosaur had very strong legs, and a powerful tail, because the muscles are huge.

The shape of the muscles shows the general outline of the body. The skin can now be added. There is no way to tell what colour dinosaurs were when they were alive. But we can look at animals today and make sensible guesses. Many large plant-eating dinosaurs were probably grey, like elephants and rhinoceroses. Smaller dinosaurs that lived in woods may have been green or brown to blend in with the trees. The very small dinosaurs might have had bright colours, like many lizards today.

Left: finally the skin can be coloured in.

13

A CHANGING WORLD
Dating the rocks

The world is very ancient and the dinosaurs lived long before the first human beings appeared. Scientists can now work out the age of the earth from rocks. They can also tell when everything happened from the very beginning of life right up to today.

As long ago as 1654, an Irishman called Archbishop James Ussher tried to work out the age of the earth. He added up the ages of people in the Bible, and decided that the earth was created in 4004 BC. But it was soon clear that this was not old enough at all.

A famous Scottish geologist called James Hutton (1726-97) saw how slowly things happened in nature. He realized it must have taken thousands

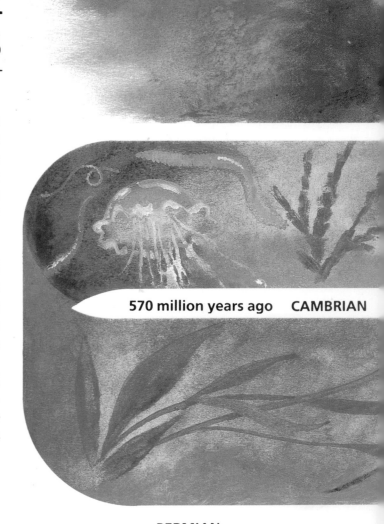

4,600 million years ago

570 million years ago   CAMBRIAN

TRIASSIC   245 million years ago

PERMIAN

JURASSIC

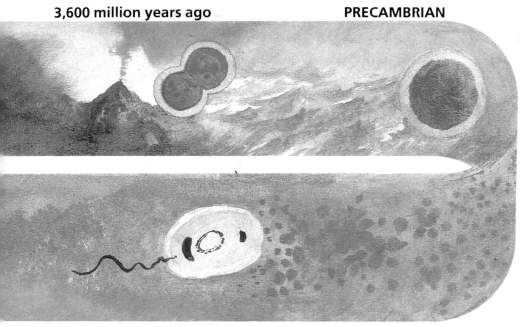

3,600 million years ago   PRECAMBRIAN

of years for the deep valleys in the Scottish hills to be worn down by streams and rivers. He also realized that the rocks must have taken millions of years to be laid down.

Rocks like sandstones and mudstones are laid down in layers, one on top of the other, like the layers of a cake. You can often see this in cliffs and quarries. The oldest rocks are at the bottom of the pile. The ages of the rock layers can be worked out by any fossils that are found, and also by using chemicals.

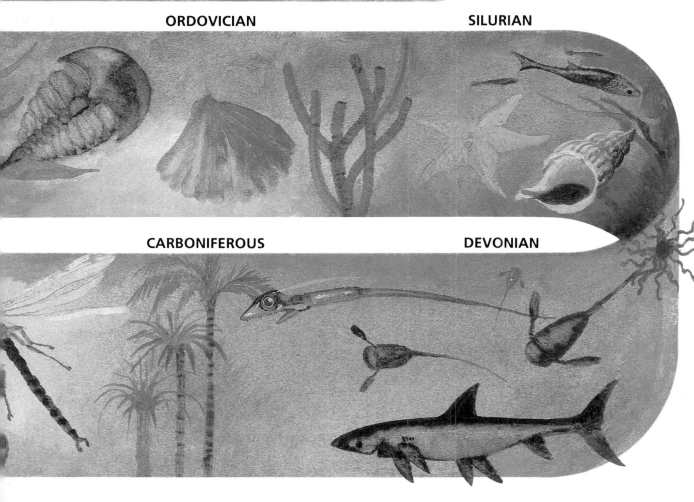

ORDOVICIAN   SILURIAN

CARBONIFEROUS   DEVONIAN

Main picture: The evolution of life. The early earth was unsuitable for life. It was hot and there was no water or air. The first life arose about 1000 million years after the origin of the earth. The first larger animals lived in the seas. These included shell fish, trilobites (with many legs), and fish. The first land animals were centipedes, spiders, and insects. The first amphibians and reptiles moved on to land to feed on these.

CRETACEOUS   **64 million years ago**   TERTIARY   Today

Life before dinosaurs

Right: the early Precambrian world had no life.

Left: early sea creatures of the Late Precambrian included jelly fish and worms.

Below: some of the earliest sea creatures of the Cambrian period were trilobites which had numerous legs.

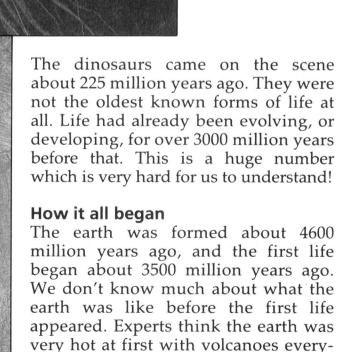

The dinosaurs came on the scene about 225 million years ago. They were not the oldest known forms of life at all. Life had already been evolving, or developing, for over 3000 million years before that. This is a huge number which is very hard for us to understand!

How it all began

The earth was formed about 4600 million years ago, and the first life began about 3500 million years ago. We don't know much about what the earth was like before the first life appeared. Experts think the earth was very hot at first with volcanoes everywhere. Gradually oceans formed, and there was lightning and radiation from the sun and space. All kinds of simple chemicals floated around in the seas. Sometimes, these chemicals joined together to make more complex chemicals. Scientists think that this is how the very first life began. They have made models of what these ancient seas might have been like. When electrical sparks go through the mixture (just like lightning hitting the sea) simple living chemicals form.

The oldest fossils of life are 3500 million years old, and they are tiny blobs or 'cells'. Cells are the building blocks of all plants and animals. They look like viruses and bacteria, which can only be seen under a microscope.

Right: backboned animals moved on to land in the Carboniferous coal forests.

Below: lizard-like reptiles lived in the Late Permian, just before the age of the dinosaurs.

Above: early fish of the Devonian period were often heavily armoured.

Life moves on land

By about 600 million years ago, many larger plants and animals were around, like shellfish, seaweeds, worms, and corals. Soon the first fishes appeared, and then about 400 millions years ago life first moved on to land. Great forests developed about 300 million years ago, and these were filled with giant flies and beetles, as well as four-legged animals that looked like lizards. Some of these were 'ancestors', or parents of dinosaurs.

The world of dinosaurs

Continents on the move

The world the dinosaurs lived in was very different from our world today. For a start, the lands and oceans have moved since then.

The inside of the earth is made of melted, or 'molten' rock. This is covered by a thin crust which is made up of separate sheets of rock, or 'plates'. Each ocean is on a plate. Each 'continent', or major area of land, like Africa, is also on a separate plate.

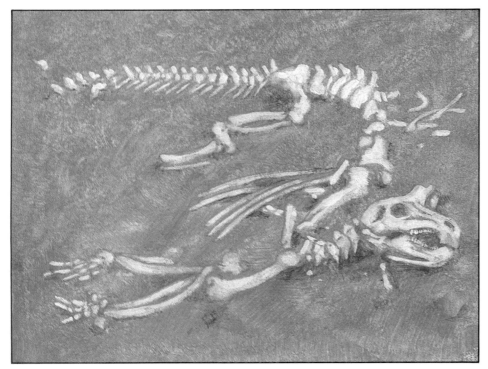

Above: the changing positions of the continents on earth. (From the back: the continents as they were 200 million years ago, 100 million years ago, and as they are today.)

Below: complete skeletons of dinosaurs are sometimes found. The bones are laid out just as they were buried in the rock.

The plates move very slowly – a few centimetres, or about an inch, every 100 years. As they move, they grind together, making earthquakes and volcanoes. When the dinosaurs had just appeared, 225 million years ago, all the continents were joined together. A big dinosaur could have walked from Australia to Canada, or from South America to Russia, without getting its feet wet! By 100 million years ago, the Atlantic Ocean had started to open up, and the continents were moving further apart. This is called 'continental drift' and it is still going on today.

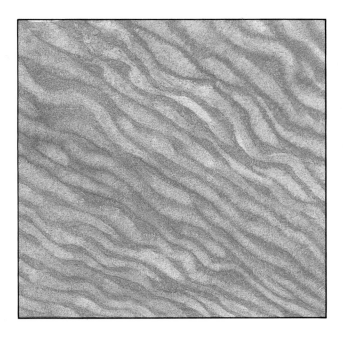

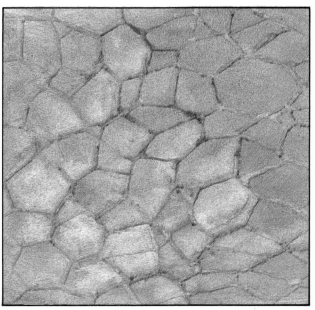

Far left and left: fossil ripple marks and mud cracks are often found, and they look just like modern examples.

Looking at the rocks

Dinosaur bones are often found in rocks from ancient rivers and lakes. When the bones are collected, geologists look at the rocks very closely to try to find out just what the world was like. They can work out the size of any rivers, how fast they flowed, which direction they were flowing, and even their temperatures.

Sometimes, geologists find marks in rocks, like mud cracks and ripple marks, which look just as they would today. Often, there are fossils of plants, leaves, twigs, and tree trunks. These details help us know what life was like in the age of the dinosaurs.

Left: if you could cut into the earth's crust you would see layers of rock. This is a view of the Morrison Formation in Utah, in the USA, showing sandstones and mudstones laid down by ancient rivers and lakes. Dinosaur bones can be seen at several levels.

The first dinosaurs

Life 215 million years ago

The first dinosaurs come from the Late Triassic period, especially in Europe and North America. Some of the best-known examples have been found in Germany and in southern England. We also know about some of the plants and other animals that lived then too.

The biggest dinosaur around at this time was *Plateosaurus*, which was about 6 metres (20 feet) long. *Plateosaurus* was probably a plant-eater. It could walk on its hind legs as well as on all fours, so it could reach into the tall trees to find leaves.

A more typical early dinosaur was *Procompsognathus*, which was smaller, only 1 metre (3 feet) long. It was agile, and ate small animals.

Other animals in the Late Triassic period were some of the earliest crocodiles, *Protosuchus*. These lived mostly on land, and ate small animals and fish. There were other smaller animals, like *Glevosaurus*, an early lizard-like form which ate insects, and the remarkable gliding *Kuehneosaurus*, which could leap great distances between the branches of the trees. There were also small hairy animals rather like small mice. These were the first 'mammals' (animals which feed their young on the mother's milk). These are our ancestors.

Key

1 *Flateosaurus*

2 *Procompsognathus*

3 *Protosuchus*

4 *Glevosaurus*

5 *Kuehneosaurus*

6 early mammal

More typical dinosaurs

Life 175 million years ago

About 50 million years after the dinosaurs first appeared many more different types of dinosaurs had come on the scene. The early dinosaurs, like *Plateosaurus* and *Procompsognathus*, had died out. In their place a whole new range of dinosaurs had appeared. Many new dinosaur fossils from the Middle Jurassic period are still being found in China and India. But some of the best fossils have been found near Oxford, in southern England.

The largest dinosaur at this time was *Cetiosaurus*, a plant-eater 18 metres (59 feet) long, and descended from *Plateosaurus*. *Cetiosaurus* was so large

Key

1 *Cetiosaurus*

2 *Dacentrurus*

3 *Megalosaurus*

4 pterosaur

5 lizard

6 mammal

that it probably couldn't stand up on its hind legs. But it could reach high into the trees because of its long neck.

There were also the first of the armoured dinosaurs, like *Dacentrurus*. These had spines and plates on their backs to fight off great meat-eaters like *Megalosaurus*. *Megalosaurus* had long sharp teeth, and it must have fed on the other large dinosaurs around.

There were also the great pterosaurs ('winged reptiles'), soaring through the sky, and feeding on insects, or diving for fish.

Colorado giants
Life 150 million years ago

By Late Jurassic times, many well-known dinosaurs had appeared.

The large plant-eaters had become even bigger. In this scene, based on the fossils collected by Cope and Marsh in the western USA (pages 8-9), you can see that *Apatosaurus* had grown to 21 metres (69 feet) long, and *Diplodocus* had grown to 27 metres (89 feet) long. These are the biggest land animals that have ever lived and they fed on soft water plants.

The plated *Stegosaurus* had evolved, from *Dacentrurus* of the Middle Jurassic of England. *Stegosaurus* had large diamond-shaped plates on its back, and four spikes on the end of its tail.

Two meat-eating dinosaurs are also shown on these pages: *Allosaurus* (which would have attacked *Stegosaurus*, but might have been too small to tackle *Apatosaurus*) and the much smaller *Ornitholestes* (which probably ate small lizards and mammals).

There was no grass when dinosaurs were around, but there were ferns and other plants. The trees were like modern palm, pine, and cedar trees.

Key

1 *Apatosaurus*

2 *Diplodocus*

3 *Stegosaurus*

4 *Allosaurus*

5 *Ornitholestes*

6 izard

England's Early Cretaceous

Life 125 million years ago

The next stage in the history of the dinosaurs is best seen in southern England, in fossil deposits found on the Isle of Wight, and in Sussex and Kent. These include the famous discoveries the Mantells made in the 1820s (pages 6-7).

The most common dinosaur at this time was *Iguanodon*, a large plant-eater that could walk on all fours or on its hind legs. It had a sharp spike on its thumb – probably used for pulling leaves from trees, or fighting.

There were also smaller plant-eaters called *Hypsilophodon*, which were relatives of *Iguanodon*. There were also

some large plant-eaters called *Pelorosaurus*, close relatives of *Apatosaurus* and *Diplodocus* from North America. *Pelorosaurus*, however, is only known from a few bones, so we cannot draw it in detail.

The main meat-eating dinosaur was *Baryonyx*, or 'Super Claw', an amazing new dinosaur found only in 1982.

Key

1 *Iguanodon*

2 *Baryonyx*

3 *Pelorosaurus*

4 *Hypsilophodon*

The last dinosaurs

Life 70 million years ago

By Late Cretaceous times, there were more different sorts of dinosaurs than there had ever been before. Most of the dinosaurs of this age have been found in North America, Europe, and Asia. But some of the best finds have been made in Alberta, Canada. These were some of the last of the dinosaurs. Dinosaurs died out 65 million years ago and why they did so is one of the world's great mysteries.

The main plant-eaters were duck-billed dinosaurs, like *Corythosaurus* and *Parasaurolophus*. These dinosaurs had broad snouts and strange crests on the tops of their heads. They had as many as 2000 teeth! So they could have

eaten very tough plants. The crests are more difficult to explain: they may have been used for signalling.

The other common plant-eaters at this time were the horned dinosaurs like *Triceratops*. This dinosaur was like a giant rhinoceros, and it probably used its horns to fight off attackers.

The meat-eaters included giants like *Tyrannosaurus*, which could eat any other dinosaur, and smaller ostrich dinosaurs, like *Stenonychosaurus*, which ate frogs, lizards and mammals.

New forms of life had also begun to emerge. Birds had first arisen in Late Jurassic times, but there were more of them by the Late Cretaceous. There were early flowering plants which later developed into our flowering plants, like roses, oak trees, and daffodils.

Key

1 *Parasaurolophus*

2 *Corythosaurus*

3 *Tyrannosaurus*

4 *Triceratops*

5 *Stenonychosaurus*

6 *Struthiomimus*

7 birds

8 mammal

THE DINOSAURS
The rise of the dinosaurs

Main scene: the Early Triassic. The early mammal-like reptiles of those days included the plant-eater *Lystrosaurus* (left) and the meat-eater *Cynognathus* (right). The early ancestor of the dinosaurs, *Proterosuchus*, swims in the background, and a related lizard-like form, *Prolacerta*, and the mammal *Megazostrodon*, stand in the foreground.

Below: during the Triassic, a new way of walking evolved. The early reptiles had a *sprawling* position (left) with the arms and legs sticking out sideways. This evolved through a *semi-upright* (middle) to a *fully upright* (right) position.

The first dinosaurs come from the Late Triassic times, about 225 million years ago. Fossils of these have been found in South America, North America, Scotland, and India.

These earliest dinosaurs were very small animals, only about 1 metre (3 feet) long. They ran on their hind legs, and would have barely been able to look over a dining table if they stood up straight. Dinosaurs were very rare animals at this time. If you travelled back to those early days, you would hardly have even noticed the dinosaurs. They wouldn't seem very important at all.

Ancestors
The most important animals of the Early and Middle Triassic included the ancestors of the dinosaurs, called 'thecodontians', and the ancestors of the mammals, called 'mammal-like reptiles'. Most of the Triassic thecodontians were meat-eaters. Some, like *Proterosuchus* from Africa, looked like tiny crocodiles. Others, like *Euparkeria* from Africa and *Ornithosuchus* from Scotland, looked like small two-legged dinosaurs.

Learning to stand up
Important changes in the thecodontians' evolution happened during the

Left: a close relative of the dinosaurs, *Ornithosuchus,* lived in Scotland, in Britain, in the Late Triassic.

Below: *Euparkeria,* from the Early Triassic of southern Africa, was a small meat-eater, close to the ancestor of all dinosaurs.

Triassic. At first, early forms like *Proterosuchus* held their legs in an awkward sprawling position, just like lizards today. Later thecodontians, like *Euparkeria,* became more upright, like crocodiles today, and Late Triassic forms, like *Ornithosuchus* and the dinosaurs, stood fully upright. This position helped them run faster and grow bigger.

All sorts of dinosaurs

Near the start of the Late Triassic, most of the mammal-like reptiles and thecodontians died out. This let early rare dinosaurs spread out and take over. The age of the dinosaurs had begun.

Species

The dinosaurs existed for 160 million years and, in that time, many different 'species', or kinds, arose. So far, scientists have discovered as many as 500 species of dinosaurs, and new ones are being found every year. There must have been thousands of dinosaur species altogether.

Groups

All of these species can be divided up into a much smaller number of main groups. For example, there are the great plant-eaters, like *Cetiosaurus*, *Apatosaurus*, *Diplodocus*, and *Pelorosaurus* (pages 22-27). These are very similar: they all have long necks and long tails, and they are huge. They are called sauropods, meaning 'reptile feet'.

Similarly, the giant meat-eaters, like *Megalosaurus*, *Allosaurus*, and *Tyrannosaurus* (pages 22-25, 28-29) all have large teeth and run on their hind legs. They are grouped together as the carnosaurs, or meat-eating reptiles.

There are 11 main dinosaur groups like this. You can see the history of each group in the diagram of dinosaur evolution. This shows that all dinosaurs came from one ancestor in the Middle or Late Triassic. Then, in the Late Triassic and Early Jurassic, this branched out into four main lines, which later branched out into another seven lines by the Late Cretaceous.

Below: dinosaurs came in all shapes and sizes, from tiny animals the size of chickens to the huge lumbering sauropods, 30 metres (100 feet) or more high.

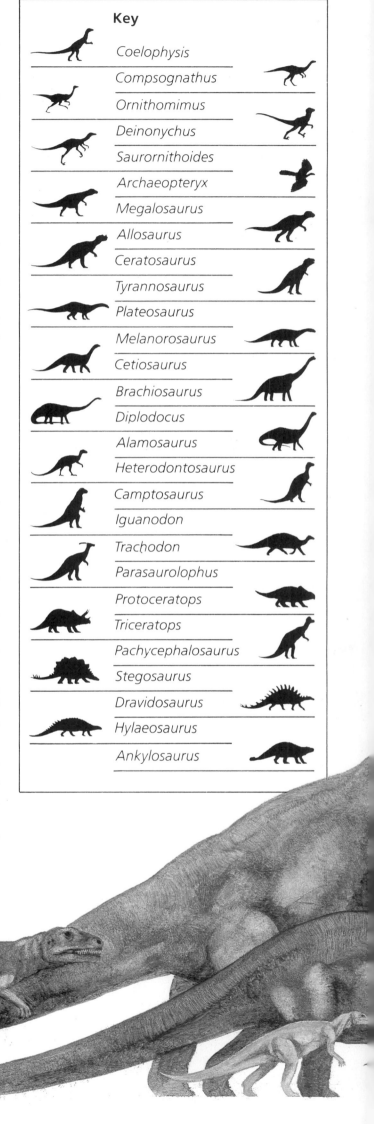

Key

Coelophysis	
	Compsognathus
Ornithomimus	
	Deinonychus
Saurornithoides	
	Archaeopteryx
Megalosaurus	
	Allosaurus
Ceratosaurus	
	Tyrannosaurus
Plateosaurus	
	Melanorosaurus
Cetiosaurus	
	Brachiosaurus
Diplodocus	
	Alamosaurus
Heterodontosaurus	
	Camptosaurus
Iguanodon	
	Trachodon
Parasaurolophus	
	Protoceratops
Triceratops	
	Pachycephalosaurus
Stegosaurus	
	Dravidosaurus
Hylaeosaurus	
	Ankylosaurus

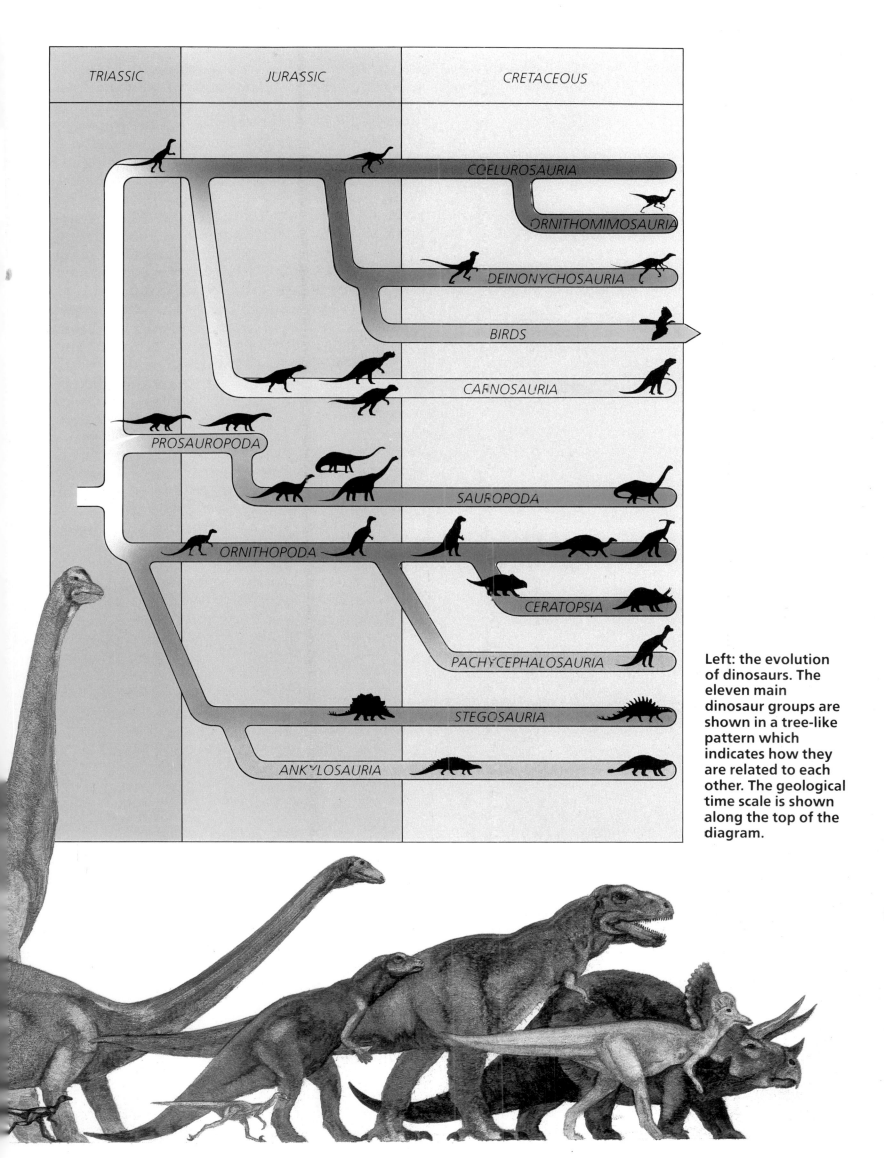

TRIASSIC   JURASSIC   CRETACEOUS

COELUROSAURIA

ORNITHOMIMOSAURIA

DEINONYCHOSAURIA

BIRDS

CARNOSAURIA

PROSAUROPODA

SAUROPODA

ORNITHOPODA

CERATOPSIA

PACHYCEPHALOSAURIA

STEGOSAURIA

ANKYLOSAURIA

Left: the evolution of dinosaurs. The eleven main dinosaur groups are shown in a tree-like pattern which indicates how they are related to each other. The geological time scale is shown along the top of the diagram.

An early meat-eater

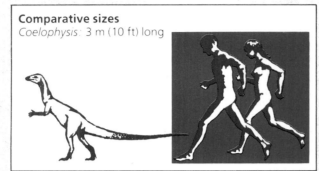

One of the oldest dinosaurs from the Late Triassic is *Coelophysis*, from New Mexico and Massachusetts in the USA.

The first of these fossils were collected in 1881. Edward Cope called it *Coelophysis*, which means 'hollow form', because the bones were hollow and very light.

In 1947, a site in New Mexico was re-excavated and at least 100 skeletons of *Coelophysis* were found there. It looks as if a whole herd was wiped out at the same time by a great flood.

There were skeletons of fully-grown animals, as well as young ones and babies. The adult was about 3 metres (10 feet) long, but most of this length was taken up by a thin whip-like tail and a long neck. *Coelophysis* was very lightly built, with long slender legs, and could have run fast. It had strong hands which it probably used to catch small animals. It had a long beak-like snout, and jaws lined with sharp teeth; just right for snapping up lizards, frogs and large insects.

Some of the adult *Coelophysis* skeletons had the bones of babies inside them. Were these babies waiting to be born, or had the adults eaten them? It seems likely that *Coelophysis* might have been a cannibal (an animal that eats its own species).

Left: the hundreds of skeletons of *Coelophysis* discovered in 1947. There were so many bones collected that the museum still hasn't finished cleaning them!

Left: the skull of *Coelophysis* has long jaws lined with small sharp teeth. The skull is lightly built, with large openings: the nostril is at the front, and the eye is the round opening second from the back.

The smallest dinosaur

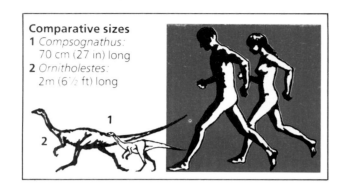
It is easy to think that all dinosaurs were huge. But some were very small.

'Pretty jaw'

The smallest was *Compsognathus* from the Late Jurassic of Germany. It was only 70 centimetres (27 inches) long and stood no taller than an ordinary chicken. The first skeleton was found in the 1850s, and it was such a beautiful specimen that it was called *Compsognathus*, which means 'pretty jaw'.

The whole skeleton showed the body lying in a twisted position in the rock. The head, and the long neck, were bent right back over the body. At first people thought this proved the animal had died in agony. But this position is often found in fossils. This is because the body of the animal dries out before the flesh rots away. The strong muscles on the back of the neck dry up, tighten, and pull the head back.

Compsognathus was a fast-moving meat-eater. It could probably have chased small lizards, frogs, and flying insects. In the first fossil found there is a lizard skeleton inside the stomach area. Before it died, *Compsognathus* must have caught this fast-moving lizard, and swallowed it whole. Like other meat-eating dinosaurs, *Compsognathus* had sharp teeth which it could use to tear flesh off in chunks from a carcass. But it didn't have any special teeth for chewing and had to swallow its food whole. In the stomach, it had some small stones which could grind the food up. This is the same with birds today, which swallow grit to help digest their food.

Below: the tiny skeleton of *Compsognathus.*

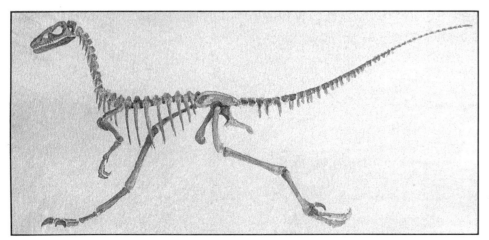

'Bird-robber'

A relative of *Compsognathus* is *Ornitholestes* from the Late Jurassic of North America. *Ornitholestes* was larger, about 2 metres (6½ feet) long. It also had a shorter snout and stronger jaws. These might have been used for cracking bones or egg shells.

It was called *Ornitholestes*, meaning 'bird-robber', because at first people thought it stole and ate eggs.

We are not sure whether this is true. *Ornitholestes* was certainly a meat-eater that could tackle quite large lizards, and even small dinosaurs.

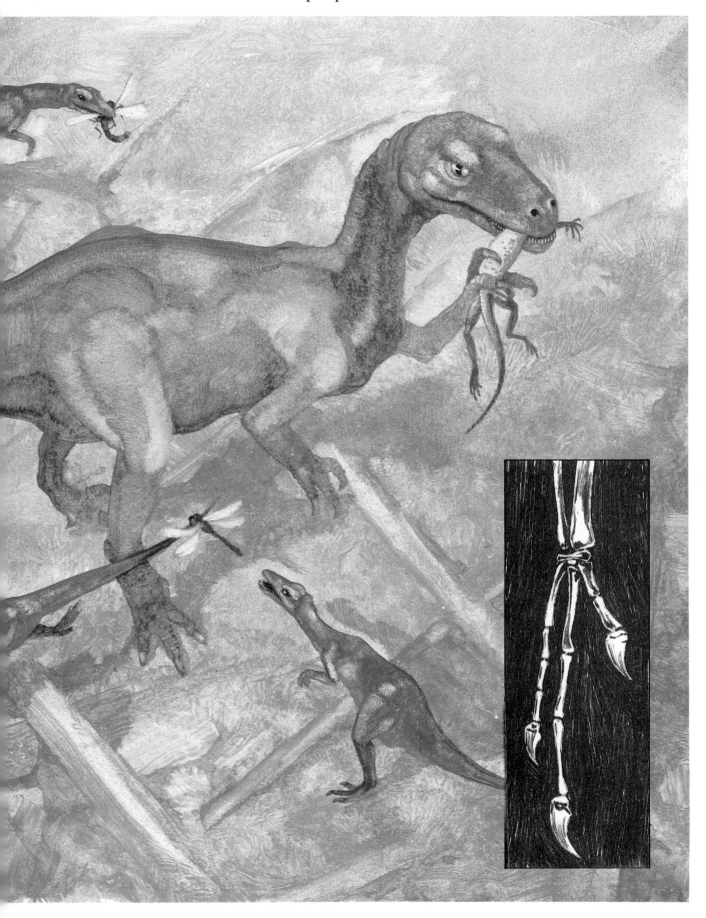

Main scene: *Compsognathus* was one of the smallest dinosaurs, and it may have fed on insects and small animals. A close relative, *Ornitholestes*, ate lizards and baby dinosaurs.

Left: *Ornitholestes* had long delicate fingers on its hand which could have been used for grasping its victims.

Ostrich dinosaurs

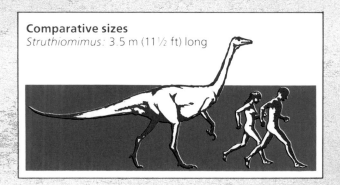

Comparative sizes
Struthiomimus: 3.5 m (11½ ft) long

A specialized group of meat-eating dinosaurs arose in the Late Cretaceous. These were the ornithomimosaurs, 'bird-mimic reptiles', or ostrich dinosaurs. The ostrich dinosaurs evolved from earlier meat-eaters like *Ornitholestes*, and they developed a lot of very special features.

A typical example is *Struthiomimus*, which means 'ostrich mimic', from the Late Cretaceous of North America.

Struthiomimus was about 3.5 metres (11½ feet) long, with a slender tail and long neck. It looked rather like a modern ostrich. The long powerful legs probably allowed *Struthiomimus* to run as fast as an ostrich, which is about 50 kilometres (31 miles) per hour. That is as fast as a race horse. The long tail was probably used for balancing. It also had long arms.

Most scientists think that the ostrich dinosaurs were not just meat-eaters but that they could eat all types of food, just as we do. Part of the evidence for this idea can be found in the skull of *Struthiomimus*. There were no teeth on the jaws at all; the sharp teeth of its ancestors had disappeared. *Struthiomimus* really had a beak; the jaw bone was probably covered by a sharp-edged sheath, just like bird

Main scene: *Struthiomimus* was one of the lightest dinosaurs, and it may have fed on insects, as well as plants.

Below: how *Struthiomimus* **would have run.**

beaks today. It may have used its beak to remove shells from nuts and seeds, or peck at tender buds and shoots, just as some birds today.

Struthiomimus had large eyes, just like birds today, and these were probably necessary for spotting its prey. The brain was probably well developed too, to allow the ostrich dinosaur to make quick decisions. It had no defences against bigger meat-eaters other than running fast. *Struthiomimus* could have run faster than the giant meat-eater of its time, *Tyrannosaurus*, and dodged its hungry jaws.

Left: the hand of *Struthiomimus* only had three long slender fingers. These may have been used for grasping food.

Far left: the skull of *Struthiomimus* is very like a bird's. The jaws are narrow, and there are no teeth. The huge eye socket near the back has a ring of extra bones in it to support the large eye ball.

Above: one idea is that the ostrich dinosaurs fed on eggs. Their strong fingers could have cracked the shells, and they could have run off quickly if the mother returned to see who was raiding her nest!

Terrible claw

Comparative sizes
Deinonychus: 3 m (10-11 ft) long

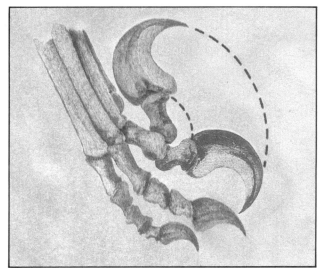

Another special group of meat-eaters arose in the Cretaceous. They were called the deinonychosaurs, or 'terrible claw reptiles'. The best-known example is *Deinonychus*, the 'terrible claw' from the Early Cretaceous period of Montana, in the USA. Skeletons of *Deinonychus* were first found in 1964, and it soon became clear that this was no ordinary dinosaur.

Deinonychus was about 3 metres (11 feet) long. It had quite a large and heavy skull compared to its meat-eating relatives. Its many sharp knife-like teeth and powerful jaws helped it to attack other dinosaurs. The hind legs were long, and helped *Deinony-chus* to run fast. It had strong arms and long fingers with sharp claws. But the main weapon was on the foot, the giant claw!

Deinonychus had only three toes on each foot. Two of these were used in walking, but the third one had a claw three times the normal size. It had to be held up because the claw would have been worn down if it touched the ground. It was very curved, and had a sharp tip. The claw could be swung downwards by strong muscles in the foot and leg. *Deinonychus* would have balanced on one leg while using the other to tear down the body of its prey with its claw. It could have dug deep into the flesh, and made a cut of up to 1 metre (3 feet) long.

Experts think that *Deinonychus* hunted in packs, just as wolves do today. The pack could attack large plant-eating dinosaurs, and slash through their thick skin. The large dinosaur would gradually weaken as blood gushed from its wounds, and the whole pack of *Deinonychus* could feast on the flesh.

Left: *Deinonychus* could swing its great claw through 180°, as you can see from the structure of the bones.

Main scene: *Deinonychus* was smaller than many of the animals it hunted, but it may have hunted in packs.

Fast thief and super claw

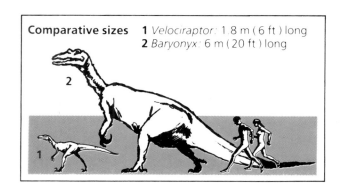

Comparative sizes 1 *Velociraptor*: 1.8 m (6 ft) long
2 *Baryonyx*: 6 m (20 ft) long

Other deinonychosaurs are now known from around the world, some quite different from *Deinonychus*.

'Fast thief'

Velociraptor, from the Late Cretaceous period of Mongolia, was much smaller than *Deinonychus*; only about 1.8 metres (6 feet) long. The first skeletons were found in 1924, and it was then realized this was a fast-running meat-eater. The discoverers thought *Velociraptor* may have robbed nests and run off with the eggs. That is why it got its name, meaning 'fast thief'.

Velociraptor was like *Deinonychus* in some ways: it had a large slashing claw on its foot, long legs and strong arms. But the head was different; it was much lower, and the snout was longer. A remarkable specimen found in 1971 shows *Velociraptor* actually attacking a small horned dinosaur, *Protoceratops* (pages 78-79). *Velociraptor* has a firm hold of the bony head-shield of *Protoceratops*, and it seems that they both died while they were fighting each other.

Main scene: a remarkable fossil from Mongolia showed a plant-eating *Protoceratops* fighting with a meat-eating *Velociraptor*. This reconstruction shows the bodies of the two dinosaurs as they may have looked when they died still fighting.

Below: *Baryonyx* was a large meat-eater with a curious long flat skull. The claw is shown here on the hand, but it could well have been on the foot as in *Deinonychus*.

Above: Mr William Walker, an amateur fossil collector, who found the giant claw of *Baryonyx*.

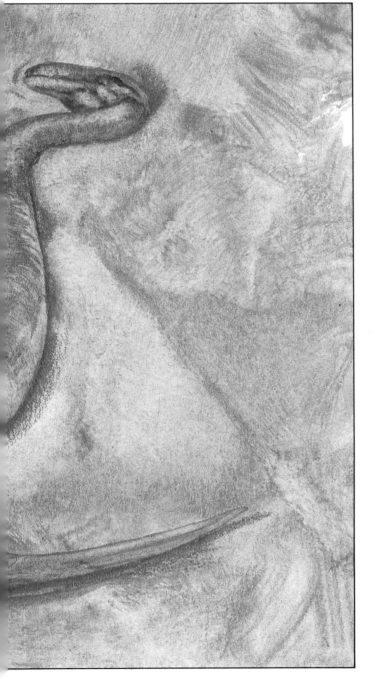

A new super claw

Another possible relative of *Deinonychus* was found in southern England in 1982. An amateur collector found a huge claw bone near London. It was three times larger than the fighting claw of *Deinonychus*, and clearly belonged to a fierce meat-eater!

Careful excavations were made in 1983, and the bones were taken to the Natural History Museum in London, where they are still being studied. The bones are in a hard sandstone that will take years to remove. But enough have been cleaned to tell us a lot about this remarkable dinosaur.

It was named *Baryonyx*, or 'heavy claw', in 1986. The claw was 31 centimetres (12 inches) round the curve. There are two theories about how this claw was used. One theory is that it slashed at other large dinosaurs, just as *Deinonychus* did. *Baryonyx* could have attacked very large dinosaurs because it was much larger than *Deinonychus*, it was about 6 metres (20 feet) long. The other theory is that *Baryonyx* ate fish and used its claw to catch them. This may seem very odd at first. But *Baryonyx* had very long flat jaws, just like a crocodile, and a skull very different from the powerful skull of *Deinonychus*. Also, the fossil of *Baryonyx* has fish scales in the stomach region, as if this was part of its last meal.

Living dinosaurs

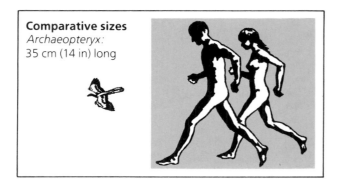
Below: one of the skeletons of *Archaeopteryx.* **It is beautifully preserved in fine limestone, and shows all the bones and feathers.**

It may be hard to believe, but birds are in fact living dinosaurs. An ordinary sparrow is a close relative of *Deinonychus* or *Apatosaurus*!

The oldest bird

The story begins in 1861 when a beautifully preserved fossil skeleton of the Late Jurassic period was found in a limestone quarry in southern Germany. It was about the size of a pigeon. Many details were preserved; and it was surrounded by the marks of beautiful feathers on the rock. This was obviously a bird. But it was odd because the bones of the skeleton were really like those of a small dinosaur.

Right: *Archaeopteryx* **could also run on the ground since it had a skeleton just like the small dinosaur** *Compsognathus* **(left).**

44

Main scene:
Archaeopteryx could
fly, and may have
perched in trees.

This new fossil, called *Archaeopteryx*, or 'ancient wing', became very famous. People saw it as a 'missing link' between the dinosaurs and the birds because it had some features from both groups. It had feathers and a special bone in the shoulder region (the 'wishbone'), just like birds. But it also had teeth, claws on its hand (in the wing) and a long bony tail, just like dinosaurs. In fact, the skeleton of *Archaeopteryx* is very like the small

dinosaur *Compsognathus* (pages 36-37). Since 1861, more specimens of *Archaeopteryx* have been found, and we now know that it evolved from a small meat-eating dinosaur related to *Compsognathus* or *Deinonychus*.

How did a dinosaur become a bird?

What was needed to change *Compsognathus* into a bird was that it had to grow feathers and wings. We don't know how feathers evolved, but they are made from the same bony material as reptile scales. The scales of a small dinosaur may have become longer and split up into hair-like strips. The dinosaur's arms would have become longer and the scales on the back of the arms would have grown longer and longer to allow the 'dinosaur-bird' to glide, and then to fly.

We are not sure whether this happened when the early 'dinosaur-birds' leapt from branch to branch in trees, or when dinosaurs which were runners jumped up into the air to catch insects.

Meat-eaters

Many meat-eating dinosaurs are not very well-known because only a few incomplete fossils have been found. Three remarkable, but puzzling, meat-eaters have been found recently in Late Cretaceous rocks of Mongolia.

'Slow reptile'

Segnosaurus ('slow reptile') was about 7 metres (23 feet) long and it had some strange features; it had no teeth at the front of its mouth, only small needle-like teeth further back. This meant it couldn't have eaten other dinosaurs,

Comparative sizes
1 *Avimimus:* 1.5 m (5 ft) long
2 *Segnosaurus:* 7 m (23 ft) long

Right: *Segnosaurus* had an unusual set of hip bones for a meat-eater. The lower bone at the front bends backwards, just as in the ornithischians (page 33).

but it may have eaten fish. The hip bones are also very strange, and show that *Segnosaurus* was not closely related to other meat-eaters.

'Bird mimic'

Avimimus ('bird mimic') is another unusual dinosaur. It was only 1.5 metres (5 feet) long, and had a skeleton like a bird, just as *Compsognathus* (pages 36-37) did. *Avimimus* also had a special ridge along its arm bones, and it looks as if a row of large feathers may have grown from the bones. The scientist who discovered *Avimimus* thinks that its arms were too short to make proper wings, so it probably could not fly.

'Terrible hand'

Another remarkable meat-eater from Mongolia is *Deinocheirus*, or 'terrible hand'. We only know about it from two enormous arms; no other part of its body has been found. Each arm is 2.6 metres (8½ feet) long, and each hand has three great claws up to 25 centimetres (10 inches) long. If the rest of the skeleton of *Deinocheirus* is ever found, it may turn out to be the deadliest meat-eating dinosaur of all!

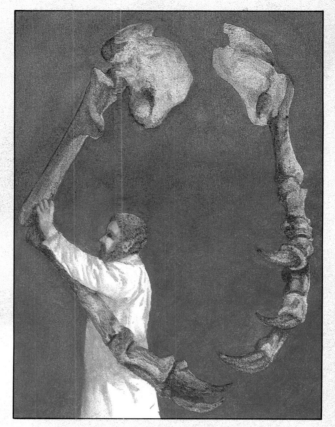

Left: the giant arms of *Deinocheirus* dwarf a human being. Imagine the size of the whole animal, if this is how big its arms are!

Main scene: the reconstruction of *Segnosaurus* (foreground) is largely imaginary, since only a few parts of the skeleton are known. The small bird-like dinosaur is *Avimimus*, which might have developed some form of feathers from its scales. However, these were probably not the same as bird feathers.

First giant meat-eaters

Megalosaurus was up to 9 metres (30 feet) long, and it was a powerfully-built meat-eater. In the original jaw bone, found before 1820, you can see the teeth clearly. These teeth were ideal for tearing flesh, and cutting it into smaller pieces for swallowing. The teeth in *Megalosaurus*, like all carnosaurs, bend backwards at the top to stop their prey from escaping. If *Megalosaurus* caught a plant-eater, every time the prey struggled to get away, the teeth would go in further.

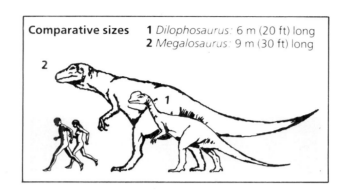

Comparative sizes **1** *Dilophosaurus*: 6 m (20 ft) long
2 *Megalosaurus*: 9 m (30 ft) long

A group of large dinosaurs, called the carnosaurs ('meat-eating reptiles') first arose in the Early Jurassic.

'Two-ridged reptile'

One of the first was *Dilophosaurus* ('two-ridged reptile'). It was called this because it has two crests on top of its head. No one has any idea what these crests were used for. *Dilophosaurus* was named in 1970 from two skeletons and other fragments found in Arizona, in the USA. It was 6 metres (20 feet) long, and could easily have attacked and eaten most of the plant-eaters of its day, like *Anchisaurus* (pages 54-55).

'Big reptile'

A more famous meat-eating relative of *Dilophosaurus* is *Megalosaurus* ('big reptile'). *Megalosaurus* was the first dinosaur to be named from remains found before 1820 in Oxford, England. Since 1820, bones of *Megalosaurus* have been found in rocks of all ages from the Early Jurassic to the Early Cretaceous of Europe, North Africa, Asia, and South America.

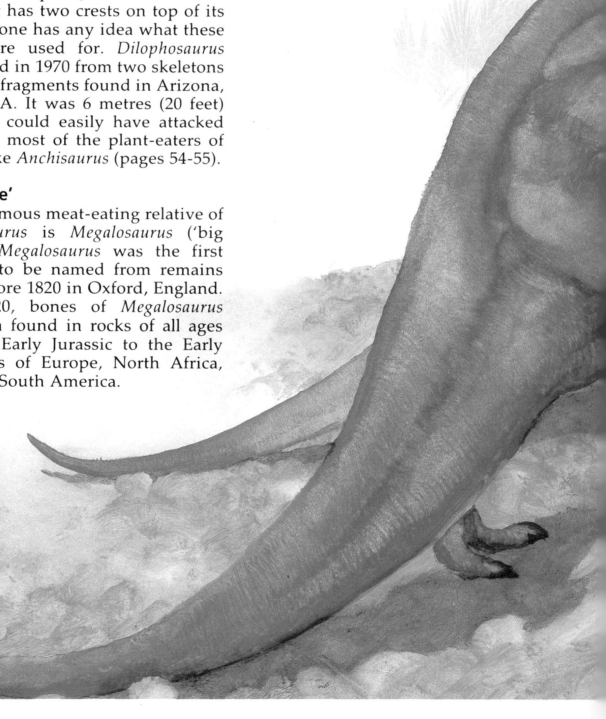

Main scene: *Megalosaurus* and *Dilophosaurus* (behind) were two of the early giant meat-eating dinosaurs.

Left: *Dilophosaurus* had a most unusual skull, with high crests on top. The teeth show clearly that this dinosaur was a meat-eater.

Late Jurassic meat-eaters

Comparative sizes
1 *Ceratosaurus*: 6 m (20 ft) long
2 *Allosaurus*: 3-12 m (10-39½ ft) long

There were two common large meat-eaters in the Late Jurassic of North America: *Allosaurus* and *Ceratosaurus* (pages 24-25).

Allosaurus was discovered in 1869 in Colorado, in the USA, before Cope and Marsh started exploring there.

Later, Marsh found more specimens and gave it its name. Major digs were organized this century, and by 1965 hundreds of *Allosaurus* bones had been collected. These are from a whole herd. Some young ones were only 3 metres (10 feet) long, while adults were as long as 12 metres (39½ feet).

Allosaurus had a long snout, and the jaws were lined with sharp jagged teeth, like *Megalosaurus* (page 49). *Allosaurus* had massive powerful legs, and feet with three large claws, and a small one at the back. The arms were much shorter than the legs, and the hands had three fingers, each with a powerful claw. *Allosaurus* is a typical carnosaur because it had massive legs, and small arms.

Ceratosaurus ('horned reptile') was smaller than *Allosaurus*, only 6 metres (20 feet) long, and it had a horn on its snout, probably to fight with.

Main scene: *Allosaurus* (left) and *Ceratosaurus* (right) fed on the carcasses of the giant dinosaurs such as *Diplodocus.* But plant-eaters like these were too large to hunt down. So the meat-eaters probably waited for the giant dinosaurs to die before eating them.

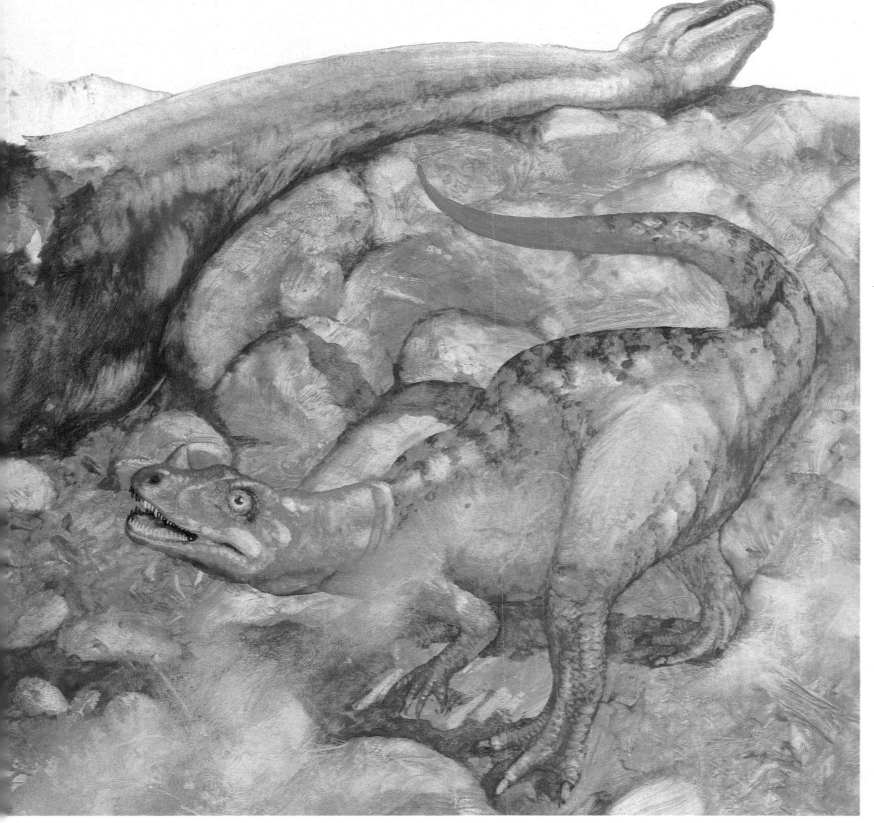

The tyrant king

Comparative sizes
Tyrannosaurus: 15 m (49½ ft) long

A famous dinosaur is *Tyrannosaurus rex*, which means 'king of the tyrant reptiles'. First remains were found in 1902 in Late Cretaceous rocks, Montana, in the USA. It was the biggest meat-eater ever!

Tyrannosaurus could reach a total length of 15 metres (49½ feet) and it stood 6 metres (20 feet) high. A man or woman would hardly have reached its knee! The head was massive, and when the jaws were opened wide, it could have bitten a human being in two if there had been any around at the time! The huge curved sharp teeth were 18 centimetres (7 inches) long: the size of a large knife. *Tyrannosaurus* had a powerful neck to hold its huge head up, and each foot had three main toes, with a small toe at the back.

The arms, on the other hand, were tiny. Each arm had two small fingers, and it is hard to see what use the arms were at all. *Tyrannosaurus* could not even reach its mouth with its hands, so the hands cannot have been used for feeding. It was suggested recently that it may have used its arms to help it to stand up. If it lay down for the night, *Tyrannosaurus* would have had a problem in the morning. It weighed as much as 7 tonnes, and if it tried to

Right:
Tyrannosaurus **might have used its short arms to help it to get up. Its head was so heavy that it needed a push at the front from the arms to raise itself.**

stand up, its giant head would keep making it lose its balance. Possibly, it threw its head back, and gave a push upwards with its small arms at the same time. This might have been enough to allow it to rock back on to its legs and stand up.

Other tyrannosaurs are known from the Late Cretaceous of North America, South America, central Asia, and India.

Main scene: the biggest meat-eater of all time on land, *Tyrannosaurus,* lived in family groups of young and old animals. They probably went out to hunt only every few weeks when they needed food.

First giant plant-eaters

Comparative sizes
1 *Anchisaurus*: 2.5 m (8 ft) long
2 *Melanorosaurus*: 12 m (39 ft) long

Main scene: the prosauropods were all plant-eaters, and they ranged in size from the medium-sized *Anchisaurus* to the very large *Melanorosaurus*.

people thought they were human! It was only in 1855 that they realized they came from a reptile. More bones have been found since then, and in places as far away from each other as North America and Southern Africa. This shows that dinosaurs could easily walk from North America to Africa overland (pages 18-19)!

Anchisaurus was only about 2.5 metres (8 feet) long, and it had a very long neck and tail. The head was small compared to the body and the small teeth would not have been sharp enough to cut up meat. *Anchisaurus* probably ate hanging plants, which it pulled down with the large claw on its thumb. It could probably have walked on its hind legs, or on all fours, because its arms were long and strong enough to support its weight.

'Black reptile'

A giant relative of *Anchisaurus* that lived in Southern Africa at about the same time is *Melanorosaurus* ('black reptile'). There is no complete skeleton so it is difficult to work out what it looked like, and how it lived. However, bones found do show that it was huge, about 12 metres (39 feet) long and it probably walked on all fours.

'Mouse reptile'

A close relative is known from South America, where a tiny baby was found recently in a nest of dinosaur eggs. The baby was only 20 centimetres (8 inches) long, and it had obviously just hatched out of its egg. Its head seems very big compared to the body, just like a human baby. As it grew up, the tiny *Mussaurus* ('mouse reptile') would have grown a longer neck and tail.

The first of the large plant-eating dinosaurs lived during the Late Triassic and Early Jurassic of central Europe, North and South America, Southern Africa, and China.

A small giant

A typical small form is *Anchisaurus*, which was actually the first dinosaur to be found in North America. When the bones were first found in 1818

Left: one of the tiniest dinosaurs is this baby prosauropod, *Mussaurus*, from Argentina.

Large plant-eater herds

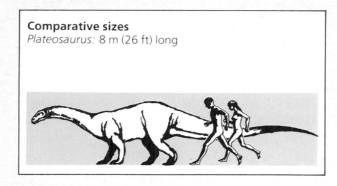

Comparative sizes
Plateosaurus: 8 m (26 ft) long

One of the most common dinosaurs in Late Triassic rocks in Europe was *Plateosaurus* ('flat reptile').

The first skeletons were found in 1837 in Germany and, since then, hundreds have been found in Germany, France and Switzerland. In some places many skeletons were found together, suggesting that *Plateosaurus* herds crossed the warm dry plains of central Europe looking for fresh plant food.

Plateosaurus is the same shape as *Anchisaurus* (pages 54-55), but much larger; about 8 metres (26 feet) long. The skull is long, and the jaws are lined with many small teeth with long roots and a leaf-shaped crown. The edges of the tooth are crinkled, but not like the sharp zig-zag edges found on the teeth of meat-eaters.

Some scientists think *Plateosaurus* may have eaten plants and meat, but it probably ate only plants. The teeth are just like those of plant-eating lizards today. Also, like birds of today, it seems to have carried small stones in its stomach to grind up the food which it swallowed.

Plateosaurus probably walked on all fours, but it could have reared up on its hind legs to reach for succulent leaves high in the trees. The hooked claw on its thumb may have been used to pull plants down, or fight.

Right: *Plateosaurus* had a large claw on its thumb which may have been used to grasp branches.

Left: *Plateosaurus* had a skull shaped like a horse's skull, but its teeth were very small. This shows that it ate soft plants.

The new plant-eaters

During the Jurassic, the big plant-eaters grew even larger. Early forms, like *Anchisaurus*, *Plateosaurus* and *Melanorosaurus*, died out by the end of the Early Jurassic. This allowed another group of large plant-eaters to emerge, called sauropods (pages 32-33).

'Volcano tooth'

One of the first sauropods is *Vulcanodon*, found in the Early Jurassic of Zimbabwe. The name means 'volcano tooth', because the bones were found near ancient volcanoes that were active when *Vulcanodon* was alive. We know it was a heavily-built animal, about 6.5 metres (21 feet) long.

Comparative sizes
1 *Vulcanodon*: 6.5m (21 ft) long
2 *Cetiosaurus*: 18 m (59 ft) long

'Whale reptile'

The sauropods became much more common in the Middle Jurassic. The first specimens were found near Oxford, England, in the 1830s. These were huge fragments of limb bones and parts of the backbone. At first, people thought they came from great fossil whales. But, by 1841, scientists realized that they were reptile bones. The name *Cetiosaurus* ('whale reptile') was chosen to show their size. We still don't know anything about the back, the neck, or the head.

Cetiosaurus was the biggest dinosaur yet; about 18 metres (59 feet) long. Its thigh bone alone is 2 metres (6½ feet) long! It was probably so large that meat-eaters of its day could not attack it.

Main scene: *Vulcanodon* from southern Africa, and *Cetiosaurus* from England, were two of the earliest giant sauropod dinosaurs. So far, complete skeletons have not been found for either of these animals.

The longest dinosaur

The longest dinosaur was *Diplodocus* which may have reached up to 27 metres (89 feet) long.

The first fossils were found in 1877 in Colorado, in the USA; a few leg bones and many tail bones. Othniel Marsh (pages 8-9) chose the name *Diplodocus* ('double beam') because of the shape of part of the tail bones. In 1899, further explorations in Wyoming, in the USA, turned up two skeletons. Scientists then learned much more about what it looked like.

Diplodocus had a very small skull compared to its body size. The snout was broad and it had teeth only at the front of its mouth. The eyes were set well back, and the nostrils were between them, on top of the head, instead of at the front of the snout.

Diplodocus had a very long neck, and it only had 15 separate neck bones. Each of these supported enormous muscles which could lift the neck up and down, and move it from side to side. The huge neck needed muscles like the steel cables on a mechanical crane to lift the head. The tail was much longer than the neck, and it had about 73 separate bones. The very end of the tail became thin and whip-like.

Diplodocus comes from the Late Jurassic of North America, and most of its close relatives, like *Apatosaurus* (pages 64-65), lived at the same time.

Main scene: the longest dinosaur, *Diplodocus*, may have fed on tall trees, or around the edges of ponds. The water would help support its great body weight.

The tallest dinosaur

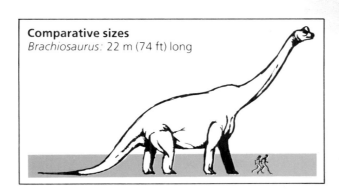

Comparative sizes
Brachiosaurus: 22 m (74 ft) long

Far right: it was once thought that *Brachiosaurus* could stand in very deep water with only its nostrils showing. However, at this depth, the water pressure would have been so great that it would not have been able to breathe.

The tallest dinosaur was *Brachiosaurus* and it reached a height of 12 metres (39 feet) when it raised its head. It could have looked over the roof of a three-storey building!

The first remains were found in 1900 in Colorado, in the USA. The name *Brachiosaurus* ('arm reptile') shows that its front legs, or 'arms', are much longer than its back legs. This allowed it to reach up higher, just like giraffes today. This also made it different from other large dinosaurs, like *Diplodocus* (pages 60-61), which had longer hind legs than *Brachiosaurus*.

Right: even larger relatives of *Brachiosaurus* (left) include *Supersaurus* (middle) and *Ultrasaurus* (right), which were named in 1985. These two are known from only a few bones.

Better skeletons of *Brachiosaurus* were found around 1910 in Tanzania, East Africa. The expedition sent back 250 tonnes of dinosaur bones! When one kind of dinosaur is found both in Africa and North America it shows that it could walk between these two places over dry land (pages 18-19).

Brachiosaurus has a short snout and a high dome on top of its head. Its nostrils are at the top of the dome, as in *Diplodocus* and many other giant plant-eaters. At first people thought this was so it could stand in deep water, and breathe with only the top of the dome showing. But this is not likely because water pressure makes it difficult to breathe in water deeper than about 3 metres (10 feet).

Main scene: *Brachiosaurus* was like a huge giraffe, with its long neck and long front legs. It could feed in high trees.

Left: *Brachiosaurus* had two very large nostrils near the top of its skull, set well back from the front tip of its snout.

The headless reptile

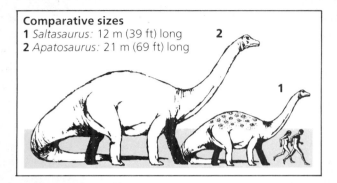

Comparative sizes
1 *Saltasaurus:* 12 m (39 ft) long
2 *Apatosaurus:* 21 m (69 ft) long

Then there was more confusion. The head given to *Apatosaurus* was wrong until 1975. Because the first skeleton had no head, Marsh guessed and paired it with a short stumpy head, like *Brachiosaurus* (pages 62-63). In 1975, scientists realized that Marsh was wrong, and that *Apatosaurus* actually had a long and narrow head like *Diplodocus* (pages 60-61). Museums all over the world had to take the wrong heads off *Apatosaurus* and fit a new one!

One of the most famous sauropods is *Apatosaurus* meaning 'headless reptile'. Othniel Marsh gave it this name almost as a joke, because the first skeleton found had no skull. Two years later, Marsh named another large dinosaur *Brontosaurus* ('thunder reptile'). Later scientists discovered the bones of *Apatosaurus* and *Brontosaurus* actually belonged to the same kind of dinosaur. The name *Apatosaurus* is now used because it was the name which was given first.

The sauropods which were the main plant-eaters in the Middle and Late Jurassic world became much less common in the Cretaceous, but some survived right to the end. One of the last sauropods was *Saltasaurus* from South America. This 12-metre (39-feet) long sauropod was unusual because it had armour plates in its skin. Its back was covered with small and large plates of bone up to 10 centimetres (4 inches) thick.

Left: the armour of *Saltasaurus* consisted of small and large plates of bone, round or square in shape.

The first bird-hips

All the meat-eating and plant-eating dinosaurs so far belonged to the Saurischia division of dinosaurs (pages 32-33). The second great division were the Ornithischia ('bird-hips'). These were all plant-eaters, and, as well as the armoured and horned dinosaurs, there were various two-legged dinosaurs.

The first bird-hips appeared in the Early Jurassic. A typical form was *Heterodontosaurus* from Southern Africa, which was only about 1.2 metres (4 feet) long. The name means 'reptile with different teeth', and was

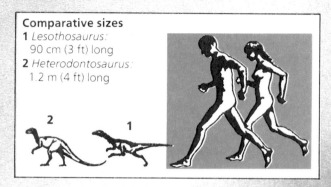

Comparative sizes
1 *Lesothosaurus*: 90 cm (3 ft) long
2 *Heterodontosaurus*: 1.2 m (4 ft) long

Right: the skull of *Heterodontosaurus*. It had three main types of teeth just as we do: nipping teeth at the front; fang-like teeth at the side; and grinders at the back.

given because it had three different kinds of teeth: there were sharp cutting teeth at the front; a pair of fangs behind these; and broad ridged teeth in the cheek region. It was a plant-eater, and used the sharp front teeth to cut tough leaves and the broad cheek teeth to crush them before swallowing.

It may have used the fangs for feeding, or fighting. It may seem unusual for a plant-eater to have fangs, but wild pigs today use their fangs to protect themselves, and to fight with rivals.

Another typical early Ornithischian is *Lesothosaurus*, also from the Early Jurassic of Southern Africa. It had small leaf-shaped teeth that were used for cutting up plant food. It was only 90 centimetres (3 feet) long and might have reached the level of a chair if it stood upright.

Main scene: two of the early bird-hipped dinosaurs were *Lesothosaurus* (left) and *Heterodonto-saurus* (right) from Southern Africa.

An early success story

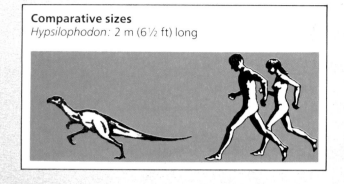

The ornithischians continued through the Middle and Late Jurassic, but only became important in the Early Cretaceous, when the giant sauropod plant-eaters became less common.

One of the first successful bird-hips was *Hypsilophodon*. Many skeletons of this fast-moving little dinosaur have been found on the Isle of Wight in southern England. The first fossils were found in 1849, and scientists realized that it was a close relative of the larger *Iguanodon* (pages 6-7, 70-71). But they were not sure how it lived.

At first people thought *Hypsilophodon* might have been able to climb rocks like a mountain goat, or even perch in trees. It had long slender toes, and some people thought it could have used these to grasp a branch, just as a bird does.

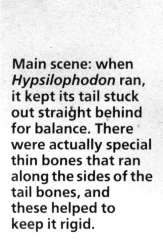

Main scene: when *Hypsilophodon* ran, it kept its tail stuck out straight behind for balance. There were actually special thin bones that ran along the sides of the tail bones, and these helped to keep it rigid.

However, recent studies of the toe bones show that it could not have curled its feet and so it could not have grasped a branch with its feet. What the feet also show is that *Hypsilophodon* was a fast runner on flat ground. Its feet were very like those of a small antelope today. It could run very fast to escape a meat-eater. The long tail stuck out straight behind, and the head straight forwards, for balance.

In the Early Cretaceous of southern England, herds of *Hypsilophodon* fed in the green forests (pages 26-27). We know about young and old animals and they ranged in length from 1.4 to 2.3 metres (4½ to 7½ feet).

Left: an early theory about *Hypsilopho-don* was that it could perch in the trees, grasping the branches with its long toes.

Left: a closer look at the foot of *Hypsilophodon* shows that it could not have used it for grasping branches. Each toe has a small hoof, and they show that *Hypsilophodon* was actually a fast runner.

Iguana tooth

Comparative sizes
Iguanodon: 9 m (30 ft) long

Main scene:
***Iguanodon* was one of the most successful dinosaurs of its day. It was a moderate-sized plant-eater, and it probably had few enemies.**

One of the first dinosaurs to be named was *Iguanodon* (pages 6-7). It was first found in southern England in 1822. Since then fossils of it have been found at about 50 places in England, as well as around the world.

One of the most famous finds was in Belgium, where over 30 nearly complete skeletons were found. The skeletons were spotted in 1878 by coal miners, 322 metres (1063 feet) under-

ground. Scientists thought at first that a herd of *Iguanodon* might have been driven over the edge of a cliff as they ran away from a meat-eating dinosaur. It now seems more likely that the herd got trapped in a muddy swamp.

Iguanodon was up to 9 metres (30 feet) long, and it stood 5 metres (16½ feet) high. It had a long snout, and its head was shaped very like a horse's. It had no teeth at the front of its jaws,

only a 'beak', used to nip off leaves. Further back in the jaws, there were lines of broad teeth used to grind up plant food before swallowing.

Iguanodon had three large toes on each foot, each with a 'hoof' instead of a claw. These were the feet of a good runner, just like a horse or rhinoceros today. It had four fingers on each hand and a sharp spike for a thumb, probably used for stabbing in defence.

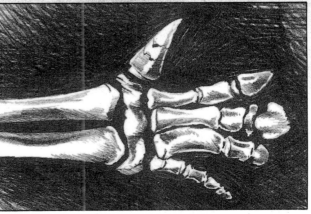

Left: *Iguanodon* had a strange spike-like thumb. Its other fingers had small hooves, instead of claws or nails. This shows that *Iguanodon* used its arms to walk some of the time.

Heat control in dinosaurs

A close relative of *Iguanodon* was *Ouranosaurus* from the Early Cretaceous of Niger, in West Africa. A nearly complete skeleton of *Ouranosaurus* ('brave reptile') was found by a team from the Museum of Natural History of Paris in 1966.

The head was large and long, just as in *Iguanodon*, and there were many teeth along the jaws in the cheek region. The rest of the body was very like the *Iguanodon*'s (pages 6-7, 70-71).

However, *Ouranosaurus* had a very unusual feature. Along the middle of

its back it had a large crest made up of long spines. On the fossil skeleton, they look just like a fence. These bones were probably covered by a layer of skin and many blood vessels. (Blood vessels are veins and arteries which send blood around the body.) The crest, or sail, was probably used for temperature control.

During the heat of the day, the large dinosaur might have become too warm. At night, when the air cooled down, the dinosaur might become too cold. *Ouranosaurus* probably used its

sail to stop this happening. In the morning, *Ouranosaurus* would stand with the sail facing sideways to the early morning sun. This way it would take in heat it had lost in the cold night, through its blood vessels. When the sun was high in the sky, it would stand with its back to the sun and lose heat as the cooler blood flowed through the skin. This happened because only the very thin back view of the sail was in the sun and the sides were in cooler shade.

Helmet head

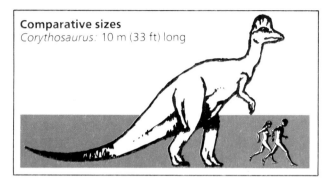

Comparative sizes
Corythosaurus: 10 m (33 ft) long

A special group of ornithischians arose in the Late Cretaceous. They developed from the earlier two-legged forms (pages 66-73) and are called the hadrosaurs, or 'duck-billed dinosaurs', or 'helmet heads'.

They were plant-eaters, and they had very broad snouts, almost like a duck's beak (which explains one of their names). Some of them also developed all kinds of strange crests on the tops of their heads.

A typical hadrosaur was *Corythosaurus* ('helmet head') from the Late Cretaceous of Alberta, Canada. This duckbill was a large animal, up to 10 metres (33 feet) long. It had a high and narrow crest on top of its head. But the exact shape of the crest seemed to be different on different specimens. So, many species of *Corythosaurus* were named. However, it now turns out that some of these were young animals and the shape of the crest changed as they grew up. Some others were males and females. Many scientists now think

Right: the duckbills had a great variety of helmet heads.

1 *Hypacrosaurus*

2 *Edmontosaurus*

3 *Corythosaurus*

4 *Kritosaurus*

5 *Lambeosaurus*

6 *Tsintaosaurus*

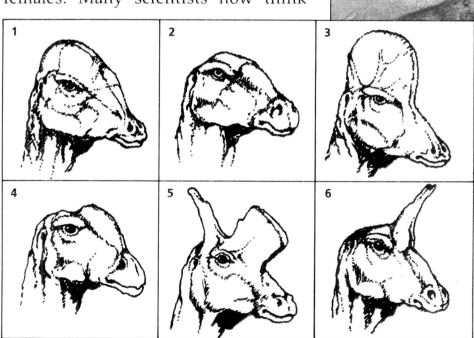

that the crests were to help them to recognize each other. There were many species of duckbills in the Late Cretaceous of North America and central Asia and all with very similar bodies. So they needed some way to tell which was another member of their own species.

Main scene:
Corythosaurus had a tall crest on its head. It might have had webs of skin between its toes which would have helped it to swim.

A snorkelling dinosaur?

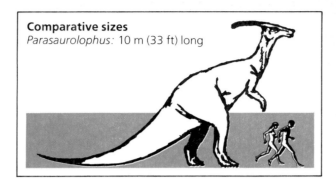

Comparative sizes
Parasaurolophus: 10 m (33 ft) long

The duckbill with one of the most dramatic crests was *Parasaurolophus*. It had a long tube which went from the back of its head and out to 1.8 metres (6 feet). We know about several species from the Late Cretaceous of Alberta, Canada. So scientists have been able to study the crest in great detail and to try to work out what this tube was for.

An early theory was that the crest was a snorkel. The breathing tubes do in fact run right along the crest. The crest is really like a long piece of piping, and the air tubes run up from the nostrils to the tip of the crest, and then back down to the throat. People thought that *Parasaurolophus* could have looked for food on the bottom of a pond with its head right under the water and still carried on breathing through the tip of the crest. However, we now know that this is impossible because there is no hole at the tip of the crest. The bone goes right across, and it could only have breathed through the nostrils on its snout.

Another idea was that the crest could be used as an air store – rather like a diver's aqualung. *Parasaurolophus* could have taken a deep breath and stored air in the tubes of the crest while feeding underwater. However, this seems unlikely because the crest was too small to hold enough air for such a large animal.

The mostly likely explanation is that the crests were to help duckbills to recognize others of their own species (page 74-75). Scientists recently made models of the breathing tubes of different hadrosaurs, and then they blew into them, just like blowing into a trumpet. And they made noises! *Parasaurolophus* could give a great bellowing noise when it breathed out through its nose. In Late Cretaceous forests hadrosaurs may have bellowed and trumpeted to find their mates.

Below: it was once thought that the crest was a snorkel and that the hadrosaurs could swim under water.

Left: the long crest of *Parasaurolophus* is made from bones from the skull roof which extend back from the nose region. But there is no hole at the end, and so it could not have been a snorkel.

The first horned-face

The two-legged ornithischians gave rise to a group of horned dinosaurs called the ceratopsians in the Late Cretaceous (pages 22-23). The ceratopsians were plant-eaters, even though many of them looked rather fierce. One of the first was *Protoceratops* ('first horned-face').

The first skeletons of *Protoceratops* were found in Mongolia in the early 1920s by an expedition from the American Museum of Natural History. These finds became very famous, partly because there were so many skeletons, but also because eggs were

Comparative sizes
Protoceratops: 1.8 m (6 ft) long

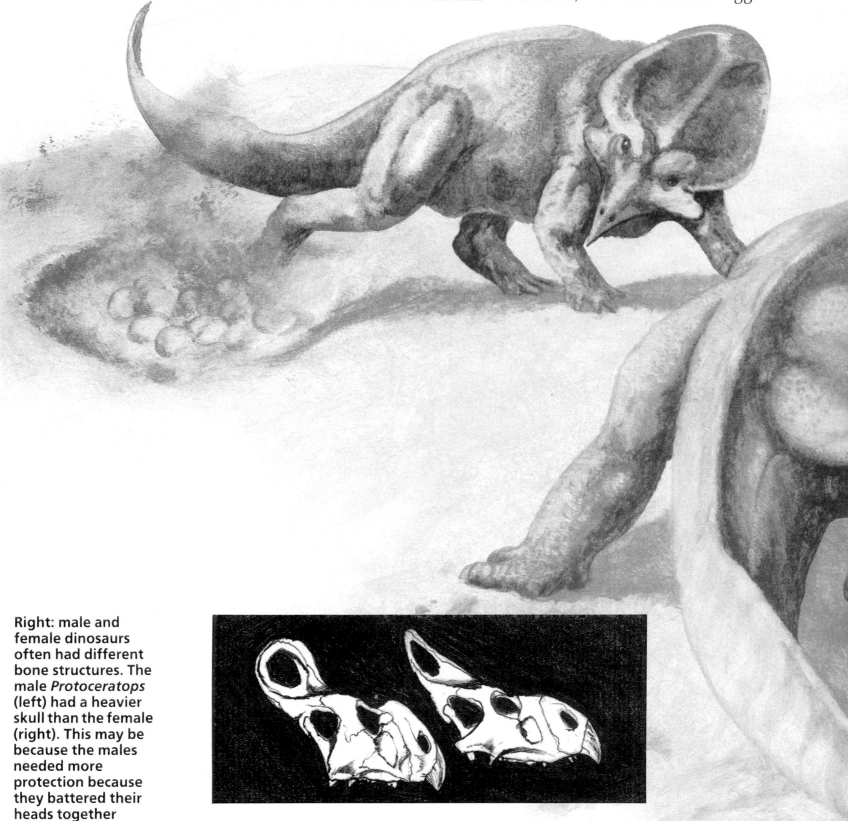

Right: male and female dinosaurs often had different bone structures. The male *Protoceratops* (left) had a heavier skull than the female (right). This may be because the males needed more protection because they battered their heads together when they fought.

found still in their nests.

Dinosaurs laid eggs, just as reptiles and birds do today (pages 96-97). The finds proved that they arranged the eggs in circles in the nest, and then covered them with sand. After some time in the warm sand, the eggs hatched, and the tiny baby dinosaurs struggled up through the sand until they reached the surface.

The exciting thing about the finds was that some of the eggs had not hatched out. The baby dinosaurs were still inside their eggs, curled up tight.

Nearby, there were skeletons of newly hatched babies, and young ones which were a few years old, as well as fully grown-up dinosaurs too. This has helped scientists to study how a dinosaur grew up.

The adults were 1.8 metres (6 feet) long, and the babies were 30 centimetres (12 inches) long. As they grew up, the bony frill over the back of the neck became larger. This helped to protect the neck from attack by fierce meat-eaters

Main scene: like all dinosaurs, *Protoceratops* laid eggs. It probably looked after its young before they hatched to keep away egg-eaters. It also probably helped the young to find food when they hatched out.

Giant rhinoceroses?

Comparative sizes
Centrosaurus: 6 m (20 ft) long

Main scene: the adult horned dinosaurs protect their young from *Tyrannosaurus* by facing outwards and using their horns.

The ceratopsians became very common in the Late Cretaceous of North America and central Asia. They ranged in size from 2 to 9 metres (6½ to 29½ feet) long. The small ones were like horned pigs, while the largest were like giant rhinoceroses. They developed different patterns of horns on their snouts, and the bony neck frill could be many different forms: long, short, frilled, or spiky.

A well-known ceratopsian is *Centrosaurus* ('sharp point reptile'). The name was given in 1904 to a new ceratopsian skull found in Alberta, Canada. It had large holes in the bony neck-frill, each of which had a long tongue of bone running forwards over it. But the first fossils of *Centrosaurus* had actually been found as long ago as 1876. Edward Cope (pages 8-9) had named these *Monoclonius* ('single-horn'). However, Cope's fossils were actually too scrappy to be identified clearly, and the name *Centrosaurus* is the one which is used.

Centrosaurus has a single large horn on its nose, and small horns over its eyes. The legs are strong, and each foot has small hooves on the ends of the toes. This shows that it could run fast when it had to, just like a modern rhinoceros can.

If a herd was threatened by a large meat-eater, such as *Tyrannosaurus* (pages 52-53), the adults probably formed a ring around the young ones, and faced the enemy with their sharp horns, just as bison do today.

Above: horned dinosaurs had a great range of different horns, just as antelope and deer do today.

Key

1 *Chasmosaurus*

2 *Centrosaurus*

3 *Triceratops*

4 *Styracosaurus*

5 *Torosaurus*

6 *Pentaceratops*

Three-horned face

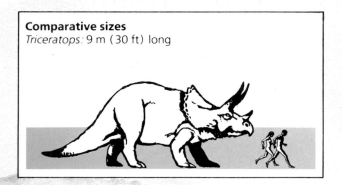

The most famous ceratopsian is *Triceratops* ('three-horned face'). The first fossils were some of its horns, which were found in Late Cretaceous rocks in Colorado, in the USA, in 1887. These were sent to Othniel Marsh (pages 8-9), who thought they came from a giant extinct bison!

More complete specimens were soon found, and they realized that *Triceratops* had three long horns: one on its nose; and two pointing forward, one over each eye. The neck-shield was large, and ran back well over the

shoulders. The back edge of the frill was made from a zig-zag pattern of knobs of bone.

Triceratops was one of the larger ceratopsians, reaching a total length of 9 metres (30 feet). It had a sharp bony beak at the front of its mouth, probably to nip through tough plants. In the cheek region, there were sharp leaf-shaped teeth, which were used to cut up leaves and stems.

Face on, the head of *Triceratops* looks very frightening. The horns could have been used to fight off attackers, like *Tyrannosaurus*, or for fighting rivals. Probably big ceratopsian males tried to frighten each other by shaking their great heads and bellowing, just as many deer and antelope do today. The males might have had ritual fights too; they would have charged each other and locked their horns together. They would then have wrestled with each other by pushing and twisting from side to side.

Left: the head of *Triceratops* as seen head-on. This is the view that would have faced a meat-eater which tried to attack!

Thick-heads

The two-legged ornithischians (pages 66-73) led to another odd little group of dinosaurs in the Mid to Late Cretaceous, called the pachycephalosaurs, or 'thick-headed reptiles'. These dinosaurs look rather like *Iguanodon*, but in fact they have incredibly thick skulls.

Pachycephalosaurus is a typical example. It was 4.5 metres (15 feet) long and is known from a skull. This shows a short snout with sharp teeth at the front of the jaws (for nipping off plants), and a row of blunter teeth in the cheek region (for chopping). The

Comparative sizes
Pachycephalosaurus:
4.5 m (15 ft) long

Right: the skull of *Pachycephalosaurus* shows how thick the skull roof was, and how small its teeth were.

Far right: when two *Pachycephalosaurus* butted each other, they crashed the thickest parts of their skulls together. This sent tremendous shocks straight through the head and down through the rest of the body.

eyes were large and set well back. But the main feature is the thickened dome of the skull.

The top of its head is very high, which makes it look brainy. However, most of the dome is just solid bone, up to 25 centimetres (10 inches) thick. So what was this thick skull roof for?

The best suggestion is that *Pachycephalosaurus* used its thick head for butting, just as mountain sheep and goats do today. At the start of the mating season, the male thick-heads would fight each other for females. They would run at each other, and crash their heads together with great force. The noise would have been like a rifle shot, but the dinosaurs were not injured because their brains were well protected by thick bone!

Main scene: *Pachycephalosaurus* head-butting must have been one of the more unusual sounds in the Late Cretaceous. The thick skull protected them, but their brains were actually very small, and there may not have been much to damage!

Early spiny dinosaurs

The stegosaurs ('plated reptiles') arose in the Middle Jurassic, and they lived in all parts of the world until the death of the dinosaurs. They ate plants, and had large spines and bony plates on their backs to protect them from the meat-eaters.

One of the first stegosaurs was *Lexovisaurus*, which is known from skeletons found in England and in France. It was a large animal, 5 metres (16½ feet) long in all, and it had about 22 bony plates standing side by side along the middle of its back. Each plate was flat and roughly diamond-shaped. It also had 12 sharp spines along its tail. *Lexovisaurus* was probably able to run quite fast (like a rhinoceros galloping) if it was chased by a large meat-eater (pages 22-23, 48-49).

Kentrosaurus ('prickly reptile') from the Late Jurassic of Tanzania, in eastern Africa, was a close relative of *Lexovisaurus*. *Kentrosaurus* had spines mainly on its back. There were about 14 small plates near the front, and 14 much larger spines stood out along the middle of its back and tail. There were also two spines over the hips which stuck out sideways.

Like all stegosaurs, it had a very small head. The skull was low and long, and the jaws were lined with dozens of small leaf-shaped teeth which were used to chop up plants.

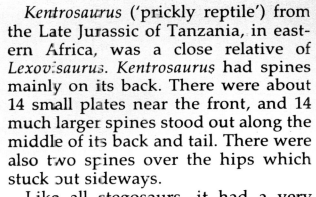

Main scene: the Middle Jurassic *Lexovisaurus* (back) was one of the first stegosaurs, and it was similar to *Kentrosaurus* (front) from the Late Jurassic of East Africa.

The largest plated reptile

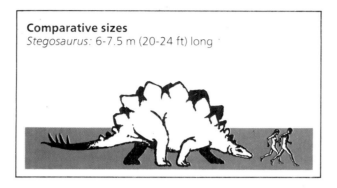

Comparative sizes
Stegosaurus: 6-7.5 m (20-24 ft) long

The best-known stegosaur is *Stego-saurus* ('plated reptile') from the Late Jurassic of North America. In the 1870s, fossil diggers found huge square plates of bone in Wyoming, in the USA. No one knew what they were. Further digs in the 1880s, under the direction of Othniel Marsh (pages 8-9), turned up complete skeletons.

Stegosaurus had rows of plates down the middle of its neck, back and tail. Just behind the head, the plates were small, but they became very large in the middle of the back, and then a little smaller down the tail. There were four spikes at the end of the tail.

Right: some scientists thought that the plates of *Stegosaurus* lay flat, forming a kind of protective shell. However, the bone structure shows that they stood upright.

Most scientists think that the plates stood upright in a double row down the back, as you can see in the main picture. But two recent theories are either that the plates were arranged in a single row, one behind the other; or that the plates stuck out sideways. It is hard to say which idea is correct because the plates were not fixed to the bones of the skeleton, but only to the skin, which is not preserved. It seems most likely, however, that the plates stood upright.

But what were these plates for? One idea is that they helped to protect *Stegosaurus* from the meat-eaters of its day, such as *Allosaurus* and *Cerato-saurus* (pages 24-25, 50-51). Another

Main scene: a young *Stegosaurus* using its spiny tail to protect itself from attack by the large meat-eater, *Allosaurus.*

idea is that *Stegosaurus* may have used the plates to control its body heat, just as *Ouranoscurus* might have done (pages 72-73). The plates were probably covered with skin which had many blood vessels, and the blood would take up heat from the early morning sun, or give off heat if *Stegosaurus* stood in the shade.

Left: it has been suggested that the plates of *Stegosaurus* stood in a single row.

Bone-skins

Main scene: *Polacanthus* (front) and *Hylaeosaurus* (back) were heavily armoured with horns and bone lumps in their skins.

Comparative sizes
1 *Polacanthus:* 4 m (13 ft) long
2 *Hylaeosaurus:* 4 m (13 ft) long

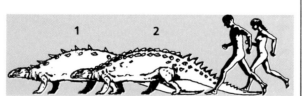

The final group of dinosaurs were the ankylosaurs, which appeared in the Middle Jurassic, and lived right through to the end of the Cretaceous.

They are probably closely related to stegosaurs (pages 86-89). The name ankylosaur ('fused reptile') refers to their armour, which was made from lumps of bone set deep in the skin and joined, or fused, together. Two typical ankylosaurs are *Hylaeosaurus* and *Polacanthus* from the Early Cretaceous of southern England (pages 26-27).

In fact, *Hylaeosaurus* ('woodland reptile') was the third dinosaur to be discovered, after *Megalosaurus* and *Iguanodon* (pages 6-7). Part of a skeleton was found in 1833, but it was only the front half of the body buried in a large block of limestone. It showed great plates and spines of bone in the skin. Since 1833, not many more fossils have been found.

Hylaeosaurus probably reached a length of about 4 metres (13 feet). It had a small head which was covered with armour-plates. The skin of the body was tightly covered with small

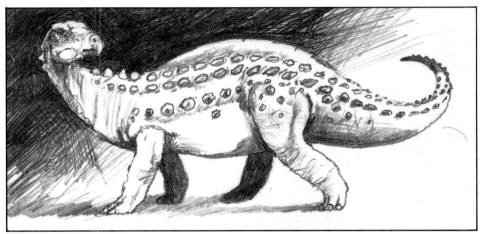

bone plates, as tough as the shell of a turtle. Set into this bony skin were a number of great bony knobs over the neck and back, and a ring of sharp spines on the tail, and around the sides. It would have been very hard for a meat-eater to attack *Hylaeosaurus*!

A skeleton of another ankylosaur from the Early Cretaceous of southern England was found in 1856, and named *Polacanthus* ('many spikes'). Unfortunately, the skeleton was just the back half of the body, so that it cannot be compared directly with *Hylaeosaurus*, which was only a front half. *Polacanthus* was about the same size as *Hylaeosaurus*, and it had roughly the same arrangement of spines and plates. Some scientists have suggested that the two forms are really both the same animal, but a new study done in 1987 has suggested that *Polacanthus* and *Hylaeosaurus* were different animals because they had different spines.

No one knows where the ankylosaurs or stegosaurs came from. An early armoured dinosaur called *Scelidosaurus* has been found in the Early Jurassic of southern England, and it looks like an ankylosaur, but it might be an early stegosaur.

Above:
Scelidosaurus **from England is the oldest known armoured dinosaur. No one can say whether it was a stegosaur or an ankylosaur.**

The biggest club-tail

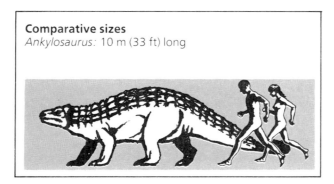

Skeletons of the biggest ankylosaur, *Ankylosaurus*, have been found in Alberta, in Canada, and Montana, in the USA. The skeleton reached up to 10 metres (33 feet) long and looked like a modern military tank, and probably weighs as much too!

Ankylosaurus had a small short head. The jaws were lined with small teeth at the back, and the front of the jaws was a bony beak for nipping off tough plant food. The skull had an extra layer of bony plates over the top, to protect the head from heavy blows. There were also four short spines around the back of the head. Its body was covered with bony plates, like other ankylosaurs, and it had bony spines around the sides and in the middle of its back.

The main weapon that *Ankylosaurus* had was a great bony club at the end of its tail. This was made from a few tail bones that had swollen into a heavy solid mass. If it was attacked by one of the large meat-eaters of its day, such as *Tyrannosaurus* (pages 52-53), it would turn its back and swing the club. The force of the blow was probably great enough to break one of the *Tyrannosaurus'* legs or damage its body. Certainly, if humans had been around in those days, a single blow from the tail of *Ankylosaurus* could have killed you!

Main scene: *Ankylosaurus* had a heavy bony club on the end of its tail. This may have been used in defence against the great meat-eater *Tyrannosaurus.* It might have swung its club from a squatting position in order to get a better swing.

Right:
Ankylosaurus had extra bones over the top of its skull for protection. Its tiny teeth show that it ate soft plants.

Left: the tail club was made from several tail bones that had fused together and expanded into a solid bony mass.

LIFE WITH DINOSAURS
Living together

Most dinosaurs seem to have lived in herds. There were young and old animals in the herd, and they moved about together looking for food. How can scientists possibly know things like these? The answer is that scientists have picked up clues which have given them proof, or 'evidence', of how dinosaurs lived.

One kind of evidence is that lots of skeletons of the same species are often found together (pages 34-35, 70-71). But does this always prove that these animals were living together? No. Sometimes fossils have been swept together into a lake, or into the curve of a river.

Better evidence has come from studying fossil footprints (page 11). Several have been found showing that dinosaurs of a single species walked together. The sizes of the footprints show how large the animals were, and so we can work out which were young and which were old animals. One set of footprints from Texas, in the USA, shows that a herd of *Apatosaurus* walked beside a lake. Smaller footprints are between larger footprints and seem to show that young animals were kept in the middle of moving herds to protect them from attack.

Right: these footprints from Australia show the large three-toed tracks of the big meat-eater, the medium sized prints of *Muttaburrasaurus* (no claw marks), and the small tracks of an animal like *Compsognathus*.

A new discovery of trackways in Queensland, Australia, tells an even more dramatic story. Scientists cleared a large surface of Mid Cretaceous rocks and found thousands of dinosaur footprints. These were made by three different kinds of dinosaurs. There are small prints made by a small meat-eater (rather like *Compsognathus*, pages 36-37), larger prints made by the plant-eater *Muttaburrasaurus* (an Australian form of *Iguanodon*, pages 70-71), and large three-toed prints made by a meat-eater (like *Allosaurus*, pages 50-51).

From the footprints scientists have worked out that the plant-eaters and small meat-eaters were feeding quietly in a sheltered hollow beneath some hills when the giant meat-eater came close. The smaller dinosaurs saw it and panicked. They ran in all directions but could not run up the slope of the hills, and had to double back and run past the giant meat-eater.

Main scene: a dinosaur stampede! A large meat-eater disturbs a herd of plant-eating *Muttaburrasaurus* and small meat-eaters (front).

Eggs and young

Dinosaur eggs have been known for some time. For example, the famous *Protoceratops* eggs and babies were found in central Asia in the 1920s (pages 78-79). But recently eggs and nests of a duck-billed dinosaur were found. They have given scientists much new information.

In 1978, a dinosaur nest and 15 babies was discovered in Montana, in the USA. They were duck-billed dinosaurs, or hadrosaurs (pages 74-77), from a new form, called *Maiasaura* ('good mother reptile'). The adult was about 9 metres (30 feet) long.

The nest was actually a mound of earth about 3 metres (10 feet) across, and with a slight hollow on top. There were pieces of egg shell lying around, which was odd because the babies were already quite large; they were about 1 metre (3 feet) long. Also they had clearly been eating plant food for some time because their teeth were worn. It was obvious that the 15 baby dinosaurs had hatched out of their eggs quite a long time before. They were probably about one year old. The amazing thing about this discovery is that it shows that these dinosaurs stayed near their nests, and probably cared for their young until they were old enough to go off on their own.

Further excavations in 1979 turned up more nests near the same site. Some of these were built over the top of older nests. This shows that *Maiasaura* mothers came back year after year to the same nesting ground. They laid their eggs and built mounds of earth around them for protection.

Bottom right: a baby *Maiasaura* in the egg. This shows the yolk sac, which is the food supply for the developing baby.

Bottom left: diagram of the nests of *Maiasaura*.

1 Top view. The nest is a low mound of earth with a circular hollow on the top.

2 Vertical section. The nests (circles) can be mapped out, and they are found close together at different levels in the rocks (a, b, c). This shows that *Maiasaura* nested in the same place year after year.

3 Side view. The eggs were laid in circles in the nest and they are still found like that where they were buried by sand and failed to hatch.

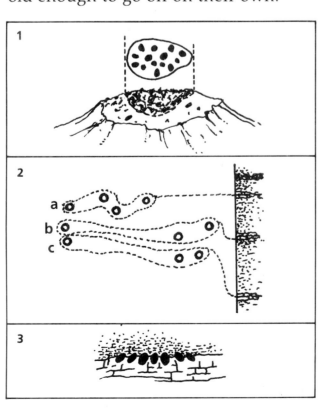

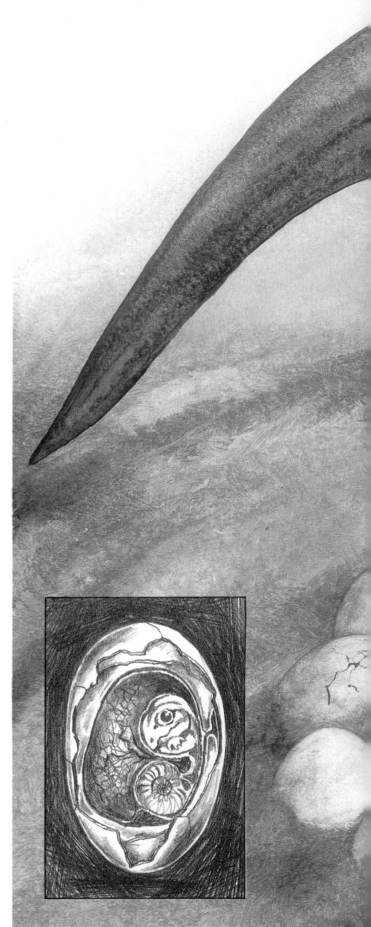

Main scene: a mother *Maiasaura* looks on while some of her young begin to hatch. The eggs were laid carefully in a nest, and the mother dinosaur probably guarded them from egg-eaters.

Flying dragons

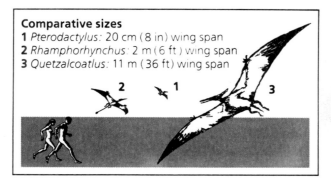

Comparative sizes
1 *Pterodactylus*: 20 cm (8 in) wing span
2 *Rhamphorhynchus*: 2 m (6 ft) wing span
3 *Quetzalcoatlus*: 11 m (36 ft) wing span

Dinosaurs were not the only great reptiles that lived on the earth. In the skies above there were the flying pterosaurs ('winged reptiles').

The pterosaurs arose in the Late Triassic at the same time as the dinosaurs (pages 30-31). They became quite common in the Late Jurassic when the typical forms, *Pterodactylus* ('winged finger') and *Rhamphorhynchus* ('narrow beak') lived in Germany. Many beautifully preserved skeletons of these two have been found.

Pterodactylus was about the size of a pigeon. It had long narrow wings made from skin which was stretched along the bones of the arms and hands. In pterosaurs, one finger on each hand had become very long, and the skin of the wing ran from this bony finger, back to the body.

Rhamphorhynchus lived at the same time. It was similar to *Pterodactylus* in most features, but it had a very long thin tail with a diamond-shaped fin at the end. This might have helped it to steer while flying.

During the Cretaceous, many pterosaurs became very large. The largest one of all was *Quetzalcoatlus* from the Late Cretaceous of Texas, in the USA. Bones of this huge pterosaur were found in 1976, and they show that it was as big as an aeroplane, and much bigger than any known bird today!

Pterodactylus had long narrow jaws with small sharp teeth, and it probably fed on insects, just as many birds do today. The fossils also show us that it was covered with hair. In some very well preserved fossils, you can see that the body was covered with quite long hair, while the wings had short hairs.

Main scene: *Pterodactylus* (lower left) and *Rhamphorhynchus* (lower right) were about the size of garden birds. They probably fed on insects which they caught in their long beaks. The largest pterosaur, *Quetzalcoatlus* (upper right) was as large as an aeroplane, and it may have fed on meat from dead dinosaurs, just like a giant vulture.

Fish-lizards

Main scene:
Ichthyosaurus could swim very fast and could have caught any small sea animal around in its day.

While the dinosaurs walked on the land, and the pterosaurs flew through the air, there were also giant reptiles in the seas. One group, the ichthyosaurs ('fish lizards') looked just like dolphins, and they were common in all parts of the world.

The ichthyosaurs arose in the Early Triassic, well before the dinosaurs came on the scene, and they were common during the Jurassic, but declined through Cretaceous times. A typical form was *Ichthyosaurus* from the Early Jurassic of Europe. It ranged in size from only about 1.5 metres (5 feet) to more than 5 metres (16½ feet) long. Many very well preserved fossils have been found in southern England, on the north-east coast of England, and in central Germany.

Ichthyosaurus had a long narrow snout lined with small sharp teeth. These teeth meshed together when the jaws were shut. It fed on fish and

swimming shellfish. Scientists know this because they have found pieces of shell, fish scales, and other remains in their stomach regions.

Ichthyosaurus swam fast after its prey, and snapped its long jaws from side to side as the fish and shellfish darted about trying to escape. It could catch the quickest of prey because of its long jaws. It also had very large eyes which helped it to hunt. *Ichthyosaurus* swam by flexing its body from side to side, just as fish do. It had a large tail fin which drove it forward very fast when it was driven from side to side. The front and back paddles were probably used for steering. Ichthyosaurs look like fish, but they were reptiles, and they had to come to the surface of the water to breathe, just as whales and dolphins do.

Above: ichthyosaur skeletons have been found in many parts of the world. The arms and legs were reduced to paddles, and the bones of the tail ran down the lower part of the tail fin.

Monsters of the deep

Comparative sizes
1 *Cryptocleidus*: 3 m (10 ft) long
2 *Metriorhynchus*: 3 m (10 ft) long
3 *Liopleurodon*: 12 m (39½ ft) long

The other main group of great reptiles of the sea were plesiosaurs ('ribbon reptiles'). They were called this because they often had a long neck and tail, just like a ribbon. The plesiosaurs look a bit like many of the lake and sea monsters that people claim to see, such as the famous Loch Ness Monster of Scotland, in Britain.

Below:
the skeleton of *Cryptocleidus* from the Late Jurassic of Europe shows its long neck and powerful paddles. It swam by moving its paddles in a great circle, almost like the flapping of a bird's wing.

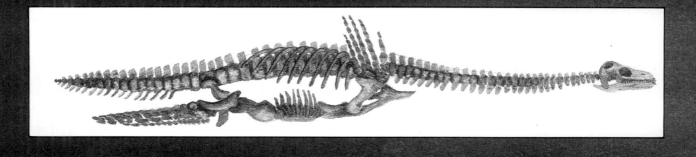

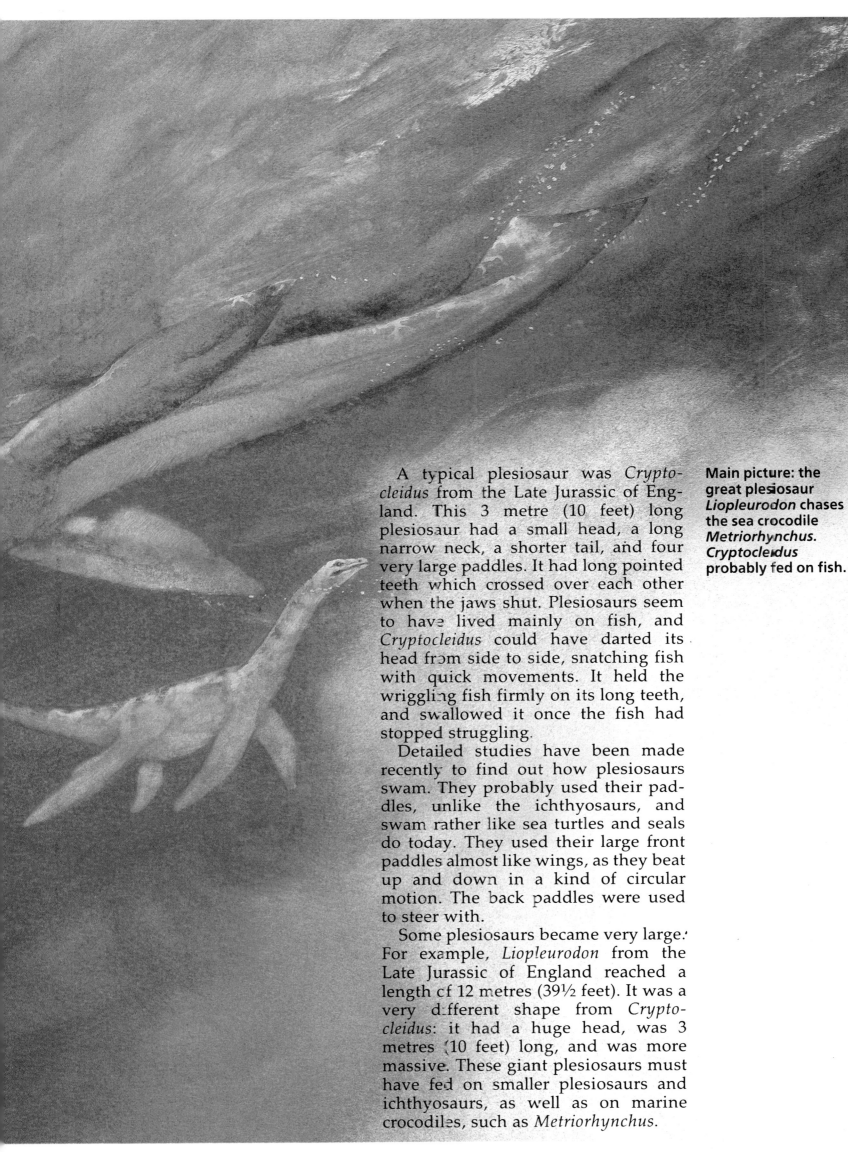

A typical plesiosaur was *Cryptocleidus* from the Late Jurassic of England. This 3 metre (10 feet) long plesiosaur had a small head, a long narrow neck, a shorter tail, and four very large paddles. It had long pointed teeth which crossed over each other when the jaws shut. Plesiosaurs seem to have lived mainly on fish, and *Cryptocleidus* could have darted its head from side to side, snatching fish with quick movements. It held the wriggling fish firmly on its long teeth, and swallowed it once the fish had stopped struggling.

Detailed studies have been made recently to find out how plesiosaurs swam. They probably used their paddles, unlike the ichthyosaurs, and swam rather like sea turtles and seals do today. They used their large front paddles almost like wings, as they beat up and down in a kind of circular motion. The back paddles were used to steer with.

Some plesiosaurs became very large. For example, *Liopleurodon* from the Late Jurassic of England reached a length of 12 metres (39½ feet). It was a very different shape from *Cryptocleidus*: it had a huge head, was 3 metres (10 feet) long, and was more massive. These giant plesiosaurs must have fed on smaller plesiosaurs and ichthyosaurs, as well as on marine crocodiles, such as *Metriorhynchus*.

Main picture: the great plesiosaur *Liopleurodon* chases the sea crocodile *Metriorhynchus*. *Cryptocleidus* probably fed on fish.

THE DINOSAURS DIE
What went wrong?

Right: one theory for the death of the dinosaurs is that a giant asteroid hit the earth and caused a huge explosion.

After ruling the earth for 160 million years, the dinosaurs died out quite suddenly about 65 million years ago, at the end of the Cretaceous period. This is one of the most important events in the history of life on earth, and also one of the most mysterious. Just why did it happen?

Main scene: were the dinosaurs killed off by intense cold when the sun was blotted out by a great cloud of black dust?

At one time, people thought that the dinosaurs were failures, and they died out because they could no longer survive successfully. But this cannot be true because the dinosaurs had lived for such a long time, and they ruled the earth. They also included the biggest land animals of all time. If you went back to the age of the dinosaurs, you would not call them failures!

Another theory is that climates were changing, and the dinosaurs could not change with them. For most of the age of the dinosaurs, the earth was warm and full of lush rich forests of tropical plants. But near the end of the

Left: one theory for the death of the dinosaurs is that climates became colder, and the tropical forests (left) were replaced by conifer forests (right). The dinosaurs could not adapt to the new conditions, but the warm-blooded mammals flourished.

Cretaceous the weather became cooler in North America, and the tropical forests gave way to conifer forests like those of northern Europe and Canada. The dinosaurs needed warmer weather, and they gradually disappeared over a time of five or six million years.

The other theory is that the dinosaurs died out very suddenly after a great asteroid hit the earth. (An asteroid is a small planet which revolves around the sun.) In the rocks at the very end of the Cretaceous period, scientists have found traces of chemicals that probably came from the explosion of a great asteroid on the earth.

The asteroid was about 10 km (6 miles) across, and when it hit the earth, it exploded and sent up a huge cloud of dust. The dust spread all around the world and blacked out the sun. This stopped the plants from growing, and so all the animals could not feed and died out.

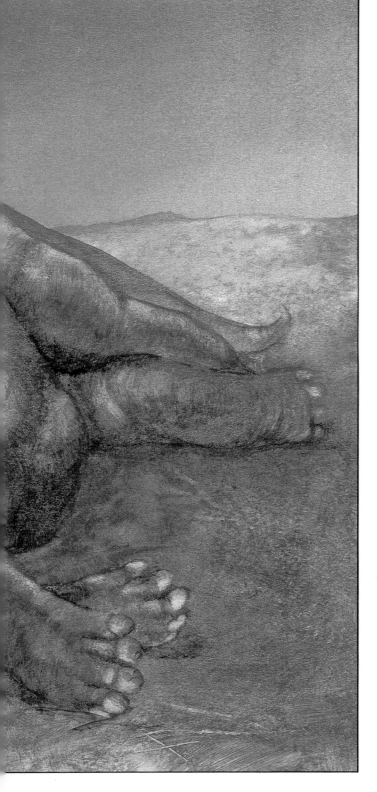

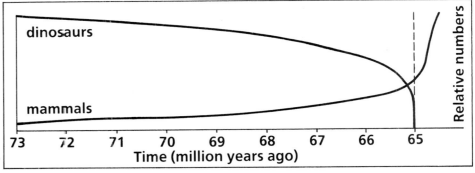

No one can say which of these ideas is correct. There is scientific evidence for both. Some say that gradual changes in climates would not have wiped out all of the dinosaurs. Others say that a huge asteroid explosion would have killed all life. But many plants and animals lived through this time quite well.

Above: the fossil finds in Montana, in the USA, show that the dinosaurs declined over 7 million years and the mammals gradually became more common.

1

After the dinosaurs

landscape: true grass had arrived. Great grassy plains spread out over Europe and North America, and herds of grass-eating mammals took over. There were hornless rhinoceroses and

The world must have seemed a very strange, empty place when the dinosaurs had all gone. There were no other giant animals to take their place right away. The forests and plains would have seemed very quiet. There were no flying pterosaurs, or ichthyosaurs and plesiosaurs in the sea.

If you looked a little closer, though, you would have seen many animals still alive. There were birds in the trees, crocodiles and turtles in the rivers and seas, frogs, lizards, snakes, and small furry animals on the ground.

These furry animals were the mammals which had been around since Late Triassic times (pages 30-31). The mammals lived beneath the feet of the dinosaurs, but they were quite small; generally no bigger than a mouse or a rat. During the Cretaceous period, some of the mammals became larger, reaching the size of a cat, but they could never become really large because the dinosaurs were around. When the dinosaurs had gone, the mammals had their chance. In the first 10 million years of the Tertiary period, which came after the Cretaceous (pages 14-15), many new kinds of mammals appeared, like the first horses, bats, and large plant-eaters.

The forests filled up rapidly. The early horses, and their relatives, were about the size of terriers, and they fed on leaves. There were cat-like meat-eaters which fed on them. In the trees above were climbing insect-eating mammals, some of which were the earliest relatives of monkeys and apes (and, of course, of humans).

On the open ground were some large plant-eating mammals, which were 4 metres (13 feet) long, and 2 metres (6½ feet) tall at the shoulders. Some of these forms had horns. It had not taken long before the mammals replaced the dinosaurs!

By about 25 million years ago, in the middle of the Tertiary period, many new forms of mammals had come on the scene: rabbits, elephants, camels, dogs, bears, pigs, and beavers. A big change had also taken place in the

long-necked camels. The largest plant-eaters were brontotheres and rhinoceroses. One of these rhinoceroses reached a length of 8 metres (26 feet) and a height of 5 metres (16½ feet) – just like a dinosaur! *Brontotherium* looked rather like a rhinoceros, but it had a strange double horn on its nose which looked like a catapult.

Left: a scene in Palaeocene times, just after the dinosaurs had died out. The mammal is *Plesiadapis.*

Left: grasslands spread in Miocene times, and large plant-eaters covered the plains. The mammal in the foreground is *Palaeolagus,* an early rabbit. The animals in the centre are *Poebrotherium,* primitive camels. The large animal on the left is a *Brontotherium,* and the small animal in the foreground (left) is *Cynodictis.*

The origin of humans

brains. Humans belong to this group: we are intelligent apes.

Humans arose about 5 million years ago. The first fossil evidence is a set of human footprints in a bed of muddy

Main scene: the Neanderthal people often lived in caves and they wore animal skins to keep out the cold. They must have met cave bears and had to fight them in order to take over a cave.

Distant relatives of humans lived at the beginning of the Tertiary period (page 106). During that time the first monkeys appeared (about 50 million years ago), and the first apes appeared (about 20 million years ago). Apes are different from monkeys because they have no tail and they have bigger ash. They were found in Tanzania in 1976, and show that a mother and child were walking along side by side.

The oldest human skeletons come from parts of eastern and southern Africa, and date from about 4 to 1 million years ago. They belong to various species of *Australopithecus* ('southern ape'). These looked like small hairy humans: they were only about 1 metre (3 feet) tall, and had smaller brains than we do. But they walked upright and had human teeth.

Modern humans belong to the species *Homo Sapiens* ('wise man'), which had larger brains than *Australopithecus*. The first fossils came from about 2 million years ago in Africa.

A close relative of modern humans lived in cold northern Europe for about 100,000 to 35,000 years ago. These are the Neanderthal people, named after the Neanderthal Valley in Germany where the first skeleton was found. They were very like modern humans, but slightly heavier. They had very large brains – often larger than we have!

The Neanderthals hunted cattle, deer, woolly mammoths, and woolly rhinoceroses in the frozen lands of northern Europe. They made clothing from the animal skins, and lived in caves to keep warm. They also used fire for cooking and for warmth. They were strong, and had excellent weapons made from stone and bone, so that they could protect themselves. They were the typical 'cave men' seen in books and films, but they were not stupid or savage. They made delicate tools from bone, and made beautiful paintings on the walls of their caves with colours from soot, and plants.

Modern humans were living in Africa and the Middle East when the Neanderthals were around. When warmer climates came to Europe, they moved there, and the Neanderthals disappeared. They then spread all over the world.

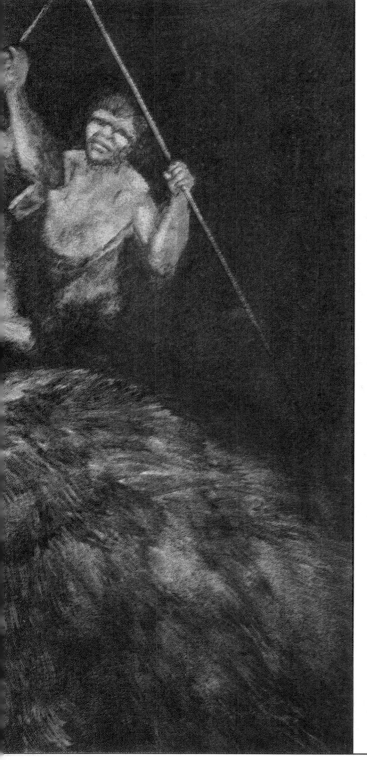

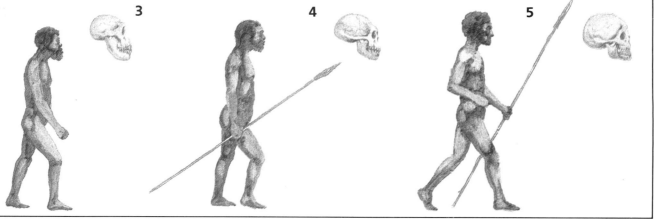

Left: five stages in the evolution of modern humans.

1 *Dryopithecus:* an ape-like form from 15 million years ago.

2 *Australopithecus africanus:* 2 million years ago.

3 *Homo habilis:* 1.5 million years ago.

4 *Homo erectus:* 1 million years ago.

5 *Homo sapiens:* 100,000 years ago, the modern human.

INDEX

Numbers in italics refer to captions, and those in bold to pictures.

♡
Kenneth
14.3.99